Choose Change...

Lauri,
Go out and create
a life you'll love.

Linda Simbers Mitchell

Choose Change...

before
Change Chooses You!

Linda Limbers Mitchell

Writers Club Press
San Jose New York Lincoln Shanghai

Choose Change…
before **Change Chooses You!**

Writers Club Press
an imprint of iUniverse, Inc.

For information address:
iUniverse, Inc.
5220 S. 16th St., Suite 200
Lincoln, NE 68512
www.iuniverse.com

ISBN: 0-595-20744-8

Printed in the United States of America

This book is dedicated to
my mother,
(Suzanna) Jane Litzinger Limbers,
who taught me that there is no such thing as can't.

ACKNOWLEDGEMENTS

First, I want to thank some special people who made this book and its contents possible. My media coach, Susan Harrow helped me get past my ego and make this book what it is today. My editor, Cathy Wilson, stuck with me through many revisions, and if it weren't for her this book would still be a file on my computer. Sharon Abla did the painstaking task of editing it for misprints and typos. She is an amazing woman and a gift from God. Christina Wolf, my photographer, met an impossible deadline.

Thanks also go to Vickie Lewis, David Goldschmidt and Chris Elias, friends and fellow coaches. Vickie pushed me to come up with more creative ways to express what I wanted to say and gave me most of the ideas for the titles of my chapters. David and Chris helped me come up with the idea for the Personality Profile in Week Eight. Jim Broome and his Sunday School Class let me "test" the survey with them.

There were several people who read the manuscript and gave me much needed input: Sadie Bolos, Jim Broome, Carol Livermore, Jess Livermore, Vickie Lewis, Tom McQueen, Paul Mitchell, and Jan Schleicher. Thank you so much.

All my life I have been blessed with wonderful family and friends. Thank you. You have been much of my inspiration. My husband, Paul put up with my long hours and late night vigils during the writing of this book. Without his love and patience, it would not have been possible. He took care of EVERYTHING while I was writing. My dad, Herbert Dale Limbers, loved me even when I made some really big mistakes. My big brother, Dale, and my big sister, Joyce, told me I was smart when I was a little girl. My little brother, Mike, moved all the way to Michigan to be with me when everyone else in my family thought I had lost my mind. My friends Carol, JoAnn and Karen, have known me through most of my mistakes, even some I did not mention here. They always loved me anyway. My son, Trey, is one of the great joys of my life and gave me a reason to keep going. My daughter-in-law, Jennifer, loves Trey, August and Hazel more than I do (if that is possible.) My grand-son, August, loves his Grammy and doesn't even care that I wrote a book. My granddaughter, Hazel, is too young to know who I am but she smiles when I hold her anyway. My stepdaughter, Anna, told me that I could do anything and I believed her. My stepson, Chris, changed his mind about me and accepted me into the family. His wife, Angela, treats me like part of *her* family. My Lord and Savior, Jesus Christ, brought me out of the pit I was in so that I could share this story with you...even if you don't believe in Him.

And finally, I want to thank you, the reader. Without you, there would be no reason to write. I hope you find several things that will enrich your life.

PREFACE

I heard many years ago that people never learn anything after the age of 16 without experiencing it personally. I don't believe that. If I did, I wouldn't have written this book. I wrote it because I consider myself an expert on the subject of change…not because of advanced degrees or education but because of a lifetime of learning. I am living proof that change is difficult. The good news is that it is not impossible.

In the past thirty-four years, I have graduated from college, and lived in three different states, all over 500 miles from the last. I gave birth to one son and acquired two stepchildren. I quit smoking at least twelve times until I finally quit for good in 1979. I have been through two divorces, fourteen jobs, and eight failed or dissolved businesses. I went from knowing about God and distancing myself from God to knowing Him personally.

Today, I am a 54 year old grandmother. I am married to a wonderful man who saw a lot of potential in me back in 1985 at our twentieth high school reunion. I have a great career as an Executive Coach, a wonderful church, fabulous friends and a loving family. This book is a result of a goal I set almost 30 years ago.

Not all of the changes I have made in my life have been easy or even good. But I certainly have had plenty of opportunity to learn about change first-hand. Hopefully, by reading my story, you can avoid some of the traffic jams and road hazards that I encountered. If you discover along the way that you need professional help, by all means seek it. At the same time, knowing someone else has survived the trip may help you through the process. If I can do it, anybody can.

And as the Classic Irish blessing says, "May the road rise up to meet you, may the wind be always at your back, may the sun shine upon your face, the rains fall upon your fields and until we meet again, may God hold you in the palm of His hand."

CONTENTS

INTRODUCTION

No matter how motivated you are, change is difficult. I discovered this in 1979. By then, I had smoked for about ten years and had quit more times that I could count. In fact I stopped telling my friends that I quit because they would laugh and ask me how long it was going to last this time.

In June of that year, my husband saw an ad in the newspaper for SmokEnders, a program on how to quit smoking. I attended a free introductory class and did not sign up because I thought it was too expensive. I tried unsuccessfully for the next six months to quit on my own. What I hadn't figured out was that because I was up to three packs a day, I spent more money on cigarettes in six months than the program cost! Thankfully there were more classes starting in the fall. I signed up, followed the course steps exactly and quit smoking on November 13, 1979, four days after my 32nd birthday.

I learned a valuable lesson during that class: *I could change!* This had a profound affect on me, but I didn't realize how profound until the following summer when I discovered that my second husband was having an affair with a friend. By then, I was teaching SmokEnders part time. One night during class a student asked me, "What's going to happen if I have to go through something stressful after I quit smoking? Won't I go back again?"

When he asked me that question, it dawned on me that I had always asked myself the same question. I realized that every other time I had quit, I was an ex-smoker, someone who didn't smoke but still thought about cigarettes all the time. I was always looking for an excuse to start smoking again. Now, I was actually a non-smoker! I was indifferent to cigarettes. It happened without my even realizing it. Right in the middle of a very messy divorce, the thought of buying cigarettes had not even crossed my mind.

That realization launched me into the journey of a lifetime. I wanted to know what happened to me that changed me so profoundly that I could not even imagine returning to smoking. So for twenty years I learned everything I could about change—reading, studying, researching. I discovered two important things. First, *most of us will not change until it is more uncomfortable to be where we are than it is to get where we want to go*. Second, contrary to popular opinion, *it takes thirteen weeks not twenty-one days to change a habit*.

> *"Most of us will not change until it is more uncomfortable to be where we are than it is to get where we want to go!"*

What happens when you get too comfortable?

One of my clients was very disorganized. He missed more of our meetings than he attended. He was constantly making up for lost time. He had become comfortable living under the pressure that this created. It took him a long time to change. His comfort had allowed him to continue his bad habits long after he could have changed. His comfort with the situation actually added to the level of difficulty that it took to make the changes he so loudly professed that he wanted to make.

You may have heard the old story about the frog. If you put a frog in some cool water, he'll be quite comfortable. If you slowly heat the water, the frog will not jump out, even if the water starts to boil, because during the slow process of bringing it to a boil, the frog adjusts. He will be boiled alive because he has become comfortable with his surroundings. Don't get comfortable! You can change before it becomes too difficult.

You don't have to wait until *it is more uncomfortable to be where you are than it is to get where you want to go!*

How long does it take you to make a permanent change?

I was taught by more that one self-help guru that it takes twenty-one days to change a habit. Because I am basically a trusting person, I believed that for years. I even taught it. However, as I started looking at the changes I made, I realized that it took me much longer than that to make any significant change. As I looked at others I knew that had made major changes, I realized that it took them much longer as well. I was curious about why many experts in the field had decided that it took 21 days.

I could find no real scientific evidence that this was true. I could not even find out who authored this thought. I had, however, some antidotal evidence that three months was a much better time frame to work with in making changes. The first case was quitting smoking with SmokEnders. While even my instructor said that it takes twenty-one days to change a habit, the class itself was eight weeks. If I counted the introductory class, which was part of the mix, that added another week. At their recommendation I continued to meet with my buddy group for another month. There you have it: thirteen weeks.

Another case was when I took the Dale Carnegie Sales Course. While other companies would profess to help you change in a weekend, they had you coming to class for thirteen weeks. I have gained some excellent knowledge from taking weekend workshops, but in the Dale Carnegie Sales Course I internalized the changes. For example, I took the class over twenty years ago. Yesterday, I was talking with a friend about the sales process and recited the five stages that I learned from Dale Carnegie: Attention, Interest, Conviction, Desire, Close. I didn't even have to get the textbook out.

> ## *"It takes thirteen weeks, not twenty-one days to change a habit."*

Finally, as a former trainer for the Franklin-Covey corporate program, I learned a powerful history lesson about Benjamin Franklin. At age 22, he was fed up with things and decided he needed more direction in his life. After a period of introspection, he wrote down a list of twelve virtues. He asked a friend what he thought of the list. His friend said it looked pretty good but he forgot humility. Reluctantly, Franklin added it to his list of virtues. He devoted one week to acquiring each virtue, and repeated the whole process every thirteen weeks.

Toward the end of his life he said, "I feel I have come to a oneness with all of my twelve virtues." What happened to number thirteen? Humility was never his. However, he did say he could fake it if he tried. The point is that he spent more than twenty-one days acquiring a life he loved. He spent over fifty years working on becoming the person he wanted to be...in thirteen-week increments.

How can you make this work for you?

In this book you will learn how to choose change before it becomes a necessity and how to do so by using the same simple process that Benjamin Franklin created so many years ago. Purchase a journal or blank book to log your journey.

You will read about thirteen principles that have helped me on this road trip called life. To get started, read the book through once. When your are done, start over at the beginning. Focus on one area each week for thirteen weeks. You will be able to do this four times per year because there are exactly four sets of thirteen weeks in a year. Imagine what your life will be like in a year...five, ten or fifteen years.

All of my coaching clients choose what they want to change. If the virtues, values, philosophies or principles I have shared are not areas that you think are important, then pick your own. At the end of each session, I get my clients to commit to take action. At the end of each week, I will give you some suggested actions. These are negotiable. If you want to do something else, that's fine; just make a commitment and do something. I will not be there to know if you made it to your destination. You may need some support from a friend along the way. Don't be afraid to ask for directions. Ultimately you have to do the work. It is your life. Go out there and create a life you'll love!

Perform a Pre-Trip Inspection

When planning a long car trip, it is always a good idea to perform a pre-trip inspection. There is a benefit to doing this. If there is anything that needs to be corrected or changed you will know before you embark on the trip. I have noticed that most people do this. I have also noticed that most people spend more time preparing for their vacations than they do preparing for their lives. In this chapter, you will begin the thirteen-week road trip toward building a life you'll love. We will start with a pre-trip inspection.

I found a love for cars very early in life. When I was four or five years old, I had a little red fire engine with a steering wheel, pedals and a bell on the hood. I remember "driving" it down the sidewalk. I thought I knew how to drive. When I was about 13 or 14, I was all too aware that I did *not* know how to drive. By then I was riding a bicycle, but I wanted to know how to drive a car more than anything in the world.

Finally, when I was fifteen, I enrolled in Driver's Ed. I was required to learn to drive using a manual transmission. I had to think about every move I made. In fact, I think I gave the instructor whiplash. But I made it! I passed Driver's Ed and I got my driver's license. At that point, I knew I didn't drive well, but I was highly motivated to learn. I practiced every chance I got. I volunteered to back the car out of the garage for every family outing. I volunteered to go the grocery store for the smallest thing, just to get to take the car out alone. I think I drove more miles the first six months with my license than I did the following six years. Now I can drive every day from my home to a client site and back and not even really remember the experience.

Broken down to the lowest common denominator, there are four stages of change that you can see from the illustration above.

- **Unconscious Incompetent**
  At three I was not aware that I did not know how to drive
- **Conscious Incompetent**
  At thirteen I recognized that I did not know how to drive.
- **Conscious Competent**
  At fifteen I learned how to drive but had to think of every step.
- **Unconscious Competent**
  Now, I can drive to a familiar place and not even remember it.

Where are you now?

Think of the last time that you had to give someone directions to get to your house. What is the first question you asked? "Where are you coming from?" You need to know where someone is starting out in order to give good directions to your house. The same concept applies in choosing change. In order to embark on this journey, you must first know where you are. Once you know that, you will never be unconscious again (Stage One—Unconscious Incompetent). This step will make you conscious of what needs to be changed (Stage Two—Conscious Incompetent).

> *"Most people spend more time preparing for their vacations than they do preparing for their lives."*

Examine the eight areas of your life. Some experts say there are three: body, mind and spirit. Others use mental, physical, and spiritual. I think that we are much more complex than that. I believe that there are at least eight areas to consider.

- Financial
- Professional
- Physical
- Recreational
- Emotional
- Mental
- Spiritual
- Relational

Each area is unique yet interrelated. Financial and Physical are usually the easiest for people to define. The others are a bit more complex. Take the following survey. At the end you will know where you are in each area.

1. Read each question.
2. Write "A" in the blank if the answer is "All the time."
3. Write "M" in the blank if the answer is "Most of the time."
4. Write "S" in the blank if the answer is "Some of the time."
5. Write "N" in the blank if the answer is "Never."
6. Ignore the box at the end of each question for now.

Financial:

- ____Do you have at least enough in savings to pay your bills for three months? ☐
- ____Do you wait 24 hours before making major spontaneous purchases? ☐
- ____Do you have a budget and stick to it? ☐
- ____Do you pay your bills on time? ☐
- ____Do you have a regular savings or investment plan? ☐

Total_____

Professional:

♦ ____Do you participate in training that will make you better at your job? ☐
♦ ____Are you at your station/desk before starting time? ☐
♦ ____Are you able to find information quickly when necessary? ☐
♦ ____Do you love the work that you do? ☐
♦ ____Do you regularly network with other professionals in your field? ☐

Total_____

Physical:

♦ ____Are you the right weight for your age and body structure? ☐
♦ ____Do you have a habit of eating well? ☐
♦ ____Do you drink at least eight glasses of pure water daily? ☐
♦ ____Are you exercising at least three days a week? ☐
♦ ____Do you get enough sleep and wake feeling rested? ☐

Total_____

Recreational:

♦ ____Do you watch less that two hours of television per day? ☐
♦ ____Do you regularly read a book just for fun? ☐
♦ ____Do you vacation for a week yearly? ☐
♦ ____Do you share recreational activities with others? ☐
♦ ____Do you spend time everyday doing something you enjoy? ☐

Total_____

Emotional:

♦ ____Do you experience true joy regularly? ☐
♦ ____Do you handle stress and bounce back quickly? ☐
♦ ____Are you able to cry when you feel sad and laugh at something funny? ☐

♦ ____Do you spend time with others sharing your feelings? ☐
♦ ____Can you handle anger appropriately? ☐

Total_____

Mental:

♦ ____Do you read books that stimulate your thinking? ☐
♦ ____Do you take classes to increase your knowledge? ☐
♦ ____Can you solve simple mathematical equations without a calculator? ☐
♦ ____Do you listen to learning tapes/CDs in the car instead of the radio? ☐
♦ ____Can you remember important names and dates? ☐

Total_____

Spiritual

♦ ____Do you believe in God/Higher Power/something greater than self? ☐
♦ ____Do you spend time alone reflecting or praying? ☐
♦ ____Do you know and review your unique purpose in life? ☐
♦ ____Do you read the Bible, Torah or other Holy Book? ☐
♦ ____Do you show compassion toward those less fortunate than you? ☐

Total_____

Relational:

♦ ____Do you have close friends/family members that you can count on? ☐
♦ ____Do you spend quality time with family and/or friends? ☐
♦ ____Are you more complimentary than critical? ☐
♦ ____Is it easy for you to say, "I'm sorry"? ☐
♦ ____Is it easy for you to say, "I love you?" ☐

Total_____

Initial Scoring "What does this mean?"

1.	Count the number of A's, M's, S's, and N's. Total number of responses equals 40.
2.	Write that number on the first line in each corresponding box below.
3.	Calculate the total points for each letter and record it on the second line.
4.	For Grand Total, add the totals from each box.

All of the time	Most of the time	Some of the time	Never	Grand Total
A's ____ X 2 = ____	M's ____ X 1 = ____	S's ____ X 0 = 0	N's ____ X -1 = -____	____

Grand total is: Ratings

70–80 You are perfect and should write a book about how you achieved this!

55–69 You are doing great and should keep doing what you're doing!

30–54 You can still create a life you'll love. Use your strengths to do so.

15–29 You may want to think seriously about memorizing this book

0–15 You should re-take the survey. I think you misunderstood the questions.

Second Step–"Where do I go from here?"

1.	Write the corresponding point value in the box at the end of each question: A=2, M=1, S=0, N=-1
2.	Total the points for each area.
3.	The highest possible score for any one area is 10.

Now that you know where you are, you need to choose your destination. In the next chapter you will work through the process of choosing where you want to be in each area.

Suggestions for Action this week:

1. Review this step at the beginning of each thirteen-week period.
2. If necessary, change the questions in the survey to match the five most significant changes you want to make in each area.
3. Notice your progress and write about it in your journal.

Target an Exciting Destination

My husband and I like to take vacations together. However, we have different ideas about what constitutes a good vacation. He likes a to be on the go; I like sit and relax. We usually take turns picking the what we do on our vacations. While it may not have a lasting impact on our lives if we choose the wrong destination for a vacation, it will have a huge impact if we choose the wrong destination for our lives. In this chapter you will investigate the destinations you can target in each of the eight areas you explored last week. The exciting part is that you get to choose the destinations!

Where do you want to go?

When I graduated from college in 1969, I thought that if I ever made ten thousand dollars a year that I would be *so* rich. Today, the Department of Labor considers that living at poverty level. Needless to say, that is not my current financial goal. However, saying I want more money is not enough. If it were, then someone giving me a dollar would be enough for me to say I had achieved my goal.

Now that you know where you are, you need to decide where you want to go. This is a very important step in the process. Without a destination any place will do. Don't get "stopped" because you don't know how to get there. You will determine that later. If you have to wait until you know every single step, you will never begin. That would be like waiting until all the lights were green between home and your place of employment before you leave for work. That may seem ridiculous but I see people doing that every day.

Once you decide on a destination, life has a way of presenting you with opportunities to get there. Remember the last time you bought a new car. Think about what happened when you were driving it home. You noticed that there were lots of cars just like yours on the road. Where were they yesterday? They were right there. You just hadn't noticed them because you were not focused on them. Once you have focused on your destination, you will begin to notice things that were available to you all along. You will become conscious of things that need to change (Stage Three—Conscious Competent). Use your journal to keep track of these things. Once you have reached your destination it will be difficult to recognize the changes you've made (Stage Three—Unconscious Competent).

To determine the most exciting destination for you, it is helpful to ask yourself some specific questions in each area. Look at the questions below. If you like, add additional questions. The answers to these questions may take some time but it is worth it. Write the answers in you journal. This is critical because you need to know where you want to be before you can move forward. Don't be afraid to think big. Pick something to work toward that will excite and inspire you into action.

Financial

♦ **Savings**
  How much would I like to have in savings?
♦ **Investments**
  How much would I like to have in long-term investments?

♦ **Debt**
When would I like to be debt free?

♦ **Income**
How much do I want to make per year?

♦ **Spending Habits**
How would I like to change my spending habits?

Professional

♦ **Career**
What would I do from "nine to five" if money were no object?

♦ **Job**
What is the most exciting job I would like to have?

♦ **Education**
What education would I like to complete?

♦ **Performance**
What habits would I like to eliminate/develop?

♦ **Opportunity**
What career/job opportunities would I like to explore/accomplish?

Physical

♦ **Weight**
What is my ideal weight?

♦ **Diet**
What would I like to eat on a regular basis that is both healthy and enjoyable?

♦ **Water**
How much water do I want to drink daily?

♦ **Stamina/Energy**
What would I like to be able to do without running out of breath?

♦ **Exercise Level**
How much and how often do I want to exercise?

♦ **Strength**
How much weight would I like to be able to lift with little effort?

- **Sleep Habits**
  How much sleep do I want to get each night?

Recreational

- **Sports**
  What sports would I like to watch/participate in and how often?
- **Movies/Television**
  What types of movies/TV shows would I like to watch and how often?
- **Books**
  What types of books would I like to read and how often?
- **Vacations**
  What kind of vacations would I like to take and how often?
- **Relaxation**
  What would I like to do for relaxation and how often?

"Without a destination, any place will do!"

Emotional

- **Peace of Mind**
  What brings me peace of mind and am I doing enough of this?
- **Support**
  What type of support do I want to get to improve my emotional well being?
- **Self Esteem**
  How would I like to view myself?
- **Openness**
  How do I want to improve my openness to new ideas?
- **Resilience**
  How good do I want to be at "bouncing back"?
- **Confidence**
  How do I want to build my self-confidence and to what level?

Mental
- ◆ **Knowledge**
  What knowledge do I want to acquire?
- ◆ **Education**
  What education do I want to complete?
- ◆ **Alertness**
  How do I want to "exercise" my mind?
- ◆ **Aptitude**
  How do I want to demonstrate my aptitude?

Spiritual
- ◆ **Clarity**
  What do I want to do to clarify my spiritual belief and philosophy?
- ◆ **Philosophies**
  What do I want to do to support my philosophy?
- ◆ **Beliefs**
  What do I want to do to support my spiritual beliefs?
- ◆ **Convictions**
  What do I want to do to live up to my convictions?
- ◆ **Reflection**
  How much time do I want to spend in prayer/meditation?

Relational
- ◆ **Time**
  How much time do I want to spend building and maintaining relationships?
- ◆ **Support**
  How much support do I want to get from/contribute to my relationships?
- ◆ **Nurture**
  How much nurturing do I want/need to give/get?
- ◆ **Advocate**
  What type of advocate do I want to be/have in my life?

How close are you to your destination?

Look at the Balance Wheel on page 20. You will notice that there are ten circles, each one larger than the previous circle. Every section is labeled with one of the areas that you just reviewed. Once you have answered the questions in each area, you will know where you want to go. The next step is to consider on a scale of 1–10, ten being the best, how close you are right now.

Not long after I set a goal to make $10,000 a year, I accepted a full time teaching position in a small school district outside my hometown. It was so small in fact that they could only pay me $3500 a year. That was not very close to my goal but it was much closer than my part-time job as a theater manager at $1.25/hour. But, income is only one aspect of finance. If I just looked at my income, I was 35% of the way toward my goal. If I took other things such as debt, spending habits, and savings into account, I was even further down on the scale. At that time in my life, I would have given myself a "two" on a scale of 1–10. I would have filled in the financial area up to the second circle.

Use this process to complete the wheel. First ask, *"Where do I want to go?" Then ask, "Where am I now?"* Follow this process with all eight areas. What is important to you now?

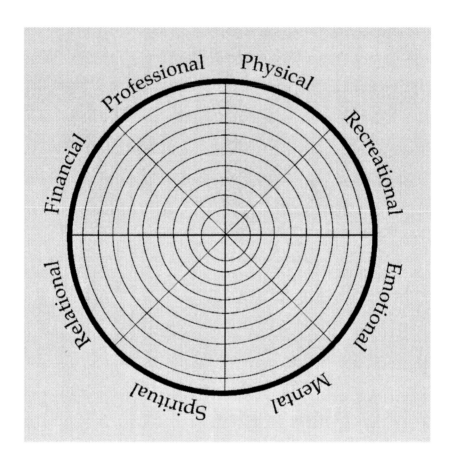

Now that you know where you are and where you want to be, you can begin the trip. It might seem overwhelming at first. Take your time. Small revisions have a way of making a significant impact on your progress. Ask yourself what is important to you now and which area will have the most significant impact on your journey. You will find that accomplishing something in one area may have an impact on another. For example, when I exercise regularly it improves my mood. Exercise comes under Physical and mood comes under Emotional.

> *"A journey of this magnitude is not completed in one day!"*

Continue the thirteen-week process by first creating the right atmosphere. Continue by choosing one area to work on each of the following nine weeks. Finish up by reviewing the the process and make changes if necessary. The idea is to choose something and begin. Don't expect to arrive tomorrow. A journey of this magnitude is not completed in one day...or even twenty-one days.

Suggestions for action this week:

1. Complete the Balance Wheel each time you work through this process.
2. Compare this wheel to your previous wheel/s.
3. Make some comments in your journal about your progress.

WEEK THREE

Pack the Right Stuff

When you take a road trip, it is important to pack the right clothes and the right gear. You don't want to spend your trip in the store searching for the items you left behind. You want to spend the time doing something enjoyable. When you pack the right stuff, you can spend your time doing that. On this road trip of life, one of the most important things you can pack is the right language...whether to yourself or others. In this chapter you will learn how to build the right dialogue to help create a life you will love.

What are you saying to yourself?

Zig Ziglar tells a story about a woman at one of his seminars who puts a cup of coffee on the floor in front of her and says to herself, "Watch me spill that!" And a few minutes later, sure enough! She spills the coffee! Zig calls this self-talk.

What did you say to yourself the last time that you made a mistake? *"Way to go, stupid!" "I knew you would never make it." "You are such a failure!"* You would never dream of saying those things to your children or a co-worker. So stop saying them to yourself.

In *What to Say When You talk to Yourself,* Shad Helmstetter, Ph.D., tells how we have heard "no" more than 148,000 times as a child. Is it any wonder that we have a lot of negative self-talk going on in our

heads? Stop right now and say these words out loud: *"I'm organized."*
Now you might be organized and respond, *"Yes, I am."* But if you are like
a lot of other people, you immediately responded with: *"NO, I'm not!"*
The next time you are about to do something, notice what you are saying
to yourself. Is it positive and supportive, or demeaning and critical?

Where did you learn to talk to yourself like that?

I used to teach in elementary school. I loved my job. Most of the people I worked with were wonderful and very dedicated. Occasionally,
however, things happened that concerned me. I remember one instance
as though it were yesterday. It was warm out, so I had my windows and
door open. I was teaching a reading class when I heard yelling coming

Correction is necessary.
Belittling is not!

from the hallway. When I went to the door to investigate, I was shocked
to realize that it was a teacher yelling at a student. She was telling him
that he was worthless and would never amount to anything. I was so
embarrassed that I immediately closed the door. I did not want to
expose my students to such abusive language. Maybe this young man
had done something very wrong, but attacking him personally certainly
did not make it better. Correction is necessary. Belittling is not.

Maybe you did not learn your negative responses from teachers but
from family members. Imagine this: a mother and father are helping
their toddler take her first steps. Mom is holding her up on one side of
the room. Dad is encouraging her to take a step from a few feet away.
She finally gets brave and steps out. Mom lets go. And we know what
happens next. She falls right on her diapers, just like every other toddler
who has ever learned to walk.

What do Mom and Dad do? They both jump up and look at her
sternly and say, *"Well, if that is the best you can do, you might as well give*

up now. You will never be a success at this rate!" Don't laugh. You probably say something similar to yourself every day.

Of course, that is not what these parents do! Instead, they scoop her up and hug her and tell her what a valiant effort it was. Then they stand her back up and start over again, encouraging her every step of the way…literally. We would think it ludicrous for a parent to treat a toddler any other way. Yet we do it to ourselves regularly. Wherever you got the notion that you are worthless, no good, or stupid does not matter. What does matter is what you do about it *now*.

It begins with a thought, which creates a feeling. Feelings form your beliefs. Your beliefs develop into attitudes. Attitudes drive your actions and give you the results you get. These results support your thoughts, which begin the cycle all over again. Therefore, if you want to change the results, change your thoughts.

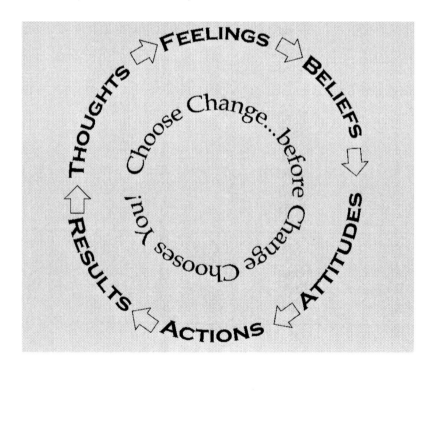

What can you do to change your thoughts?

You can accept your self-talk or change it. It is not easy but it is simple. Here is how you can do it.

Take note of what you say and change it. What do you say to yourself if you:

- ♦ Are late for an appointment/work?
- ♦ Miss a meeting?
- ♦ Forget someone's name, birthday, address, phone number, etc.?
- ♦ Spill something?
- ♦ Break something?
- ♦ Leave something that you need at home?
- ♦ Get a parking or speeding ticket?
- ♦ Gain weight?
- ♦ Can't balance your checkbook?
- ♦ Put something together wrong?

Every time you hear yourself make any kind of disparaging remark to yourself about yourself, stop. Write it down. Next, write what you would say to a close friend or family member if he or she made a mistake. With this type of self-encouragement, you'll begin to see a difference in what you say to yourself.

Notice when you do it right. I know a lot of people who constantly say, *"I never remember names."* Stop saying that! Start saying, *"I am getting better at remembering names."* There *are* times when you remember names. Start noticing those times and keep track of them instead of keeping track of the times you don't remember names.

If you use the words "never" and "always" when referring to your mistakes, stop. No one "always" makes a mistake or "never" gets it right. There *are* times you do it right. Make a list of the things you do well, correct, or right. Keep it with you. Read it when you begin to berate yourself for making a mistake.

This technique works on any negative self-talk habit you have. If you were to make a list of all the things you say to yourself that you would like to eliminate, you would be surprised at how many you have. It may take some time to overcome negative self-talk, but it is worth it.

When I confronted one of my clients about the negative things she kept saying about herself, she told me that she was just being realistic. She said that she had just made a mistake and was admitting it. I think that is a great idea. Admitting your mistakes is admirable. Dwelling on them is not. You can admit your mistakes and then notice how much you are doing to correct them.

Think about it! What you say to yourself in these situations may be one reason that you keep doing the same things over and over again. If you want to change, you need to change what you say to yourself. Keep in mind, you may have been doing this negative self-talk for so long that you will find it difficult to even recognize that you are doing it. It will take some time and effort but it is possible. Positive *thinking* is not enough. It's positive *believing* that makes a difference.

What tape do you want to play?

I like to take tapes with me whenever I drive. It is much more enjoyable for me to listen to something of my choosing. The tape deck doesn't care what I play. Your brain is like that. It will accept any tape you put in it. The problem is that sometimes you don't make a conscious choice about what tape you are playing in your head. You are probably Unconscious Incompetent. Now that I have shared this concept with you, you can move right into the Conscious Competent Stage. You can begin to make new choices.

Reject the old negative tapes. I had a friend that was working with some young men who were in reform school. He had heard of this concept and asked these boys if any of them had ever heard things like: *"You're worthless." or "You'll probably end up in jail."* One hundred percent of them had heard something like that from as early as they could remember. As a result they had played that tape in their heads over and over until they began to believe it. If self-talk can work in a negative way, then it can work in a positive way as well.

There are other young men who heard the same comments, yet did not turn out this way because they refused to believe the negative comments. They played a different tape. Most of them will tell you that they had someone in their lives that gave them a different message. They chose to play that positive tape instead. Even if you did not have someone to give you a positive message you can choose to play a positive tape starting right now.

Imagine a little girl about three years old at the grocery store with her mother. She is walking along holding her mother's little finger. Down the aisle comes Mrs. Jones who lives in the neighborhood. She hasn't seen Margaret in months and Margaret doesn't remember her at all. Mrs. Jones comes rushing up to mother and daughter saying, *"Oh my goodness! Look how big you've gotten, little lady."* And she reaches out to pat Margaret's head. Margaret runs behind her mother.

"Don't mind her," Mom says. *"She's shy."* Mom doesn't really mean that but she is trying to save Mrs. Jones' feelings. This happens often enough for Margaret to begin to believe that she is actually shy. As she grows up and goes off to school, she is faced with a lot of new people, people she has never met before.

One day on the playground she sees some other little girls playing hopscotch. She goes over and asks to play. They look at her and say, *"Who are you? We don't know you. Go away and play with someone else."* Because she is so shy, Margaret just goes over to the fence and watches as all the other children enjoy recess.

Finally, Margaret makes it to high school. She is very smart and makes good grades but doesn't have many friends. She is never asked for a date and doesn't go to any activities alone because she is so shy. Eventually, Margaret graduates and goes on to college where everything is pretty much the same. She doesn't have many friends and she spends a lot of time alone.

Once she finishes college she gets a job. She still doesn't have many friends. She may even try some new things occasionally but she never risks making friends because she is so shy. What a sad story. It is such a shame because Margaret could have played another tape.

Play a positive tape. Imagine another little girl. Her name is Ruth. She is in the same grocery store walking down the isle holding her mother's little finger. Here comes Mrs. Jones again. *"Oh my goodness! Look how big you've gotten, little lady."* You guessed it, Ruth runs behind her mother.

The difference is that Ruth's mom picks her up and says," *It's okay, Sweetie. You just don't remember Mrs. Jones. She lives right down the street. I know mommy told you not to talk to strangers but it's okay. Mrs. Jones is a friend."* Then to Mrs. Jones, *"You will really like Ruth when you get to know her. She is really a friendly little girl."* Mrs. Jones smiles and pats Ruth on the head.

One day, Ruth also goes off to school. She also sees some girls playing hopscotch. She asks to play and they say, *"Who are you? We don't know you. Go away and play with someone else."* But because she is a friendly little girl she does exactly what they suggest. This time, however, she finds some other friendly little girls. They invite her to play and she begins to make some new friends.

When she goes on to high school and college, she makes lots of friends as well. She may not be the Homecoming Queen or a cheerleader but she is in lots of clubs and enjoys herself very much. Once she finally gets a job she continues to make friends. Her life is full.

While these two examples are the extreme, there are people who have lived similar lives. Is Margaret destined to remain the same? Only if she keeps playing that old tape. She can make a new tape. At first she may not be able to call herself friendly but she can say, *"I am looking forward to having more friends. I am willing to take a risk."* Margaret can have different results by playing a different tape and so can you.

> *"Positive thinking is not enough. It's positive believing that makes a difference."*

Record a new tape. Making a recording can be very effective. Once you realize the negative things you have been saying to yourself, you can turn those around. Write the negative things you catch yourself saying in your journal. Next, write a positive statement that contradicts the negative one. For example: You are running late for an appointment. In the past you might have said, *"You are always late."* Write that down and then think of something you can say instead. *"I am always on time."* Write several statements that support the new habit you want to create. Review each statement and add some emotional words. *"I enjoy being on time. It is so relaxing to have some extra time before I have to be in a meeting."* It is like painting a word picture of the way you want it to be.

When I teach this concept in workshops there is usually someone who says, *"Linda, that is not true. I am not on time. The truth is that I am always late."* If you have a hard time saying these things to yourself because they are not true, then think of it as telling the truth in advance. If you want to change your results, change your thoughts.

One way to change your thoughts is to listen to a recording of yourself. Read these positive statements aloud a few times before you start taping. Put some emotion behind your words. Make a tape for every statement that you want to change. Play the tapes often. If you have a tape player in your car, that is a great place to listen. Play it in the morning while you are getting ready for work. It is a lot more productive than listening to the news or weather.

Keep it up until you automatically say the new phrase every time instead of the old one. It may take a long time if you have been *"playing the old tapes"* for a long time. As you change what you say to yourself in one situation, it will be easier to change what you say in the next. No matter how long it takes, it is worth it.

Since you are what you think about, you can begin by recognizing your negative self-talk. Once you recognize it, you can turn it around by changing what you say to yourself. Making a recording of the new things you want to say to yourself will increase your success. Positive *thinking* is not enough. It's positive *believing* that makes a difference.

What does your language have to do with how you live?

John Knight, a fellow author and good friend, wrote a book called *Change Your Conversation; Change Your Life.* In his book he gives several examples of how people have changed their lives by changing their conversations. He refers to negative conversation as a way to create a small box in which to live. He encourages his readers to create a bigger box by changing their conversations.

Here is one of my favorite stories from his book:

> My home office overlooks a beautiful terraced rock garden with many bird feeders. When I first placed the bird feeders in the trees the squirrels came and ate me out of house and home. I got so angry. The squirrels were these awful little greedy rats with fluffy tails that ate my bird food. Everyday I looked out at this magnificent garden and all I saw were the squirrels. My conversation with anyone who would listen, including myself, was that squirrels were greedy little rats. Sitting in my office turned into an unhappy event day after day. If the squirrels would just leave, all would be happy in my life.
>
> Something had to change. Then it hit me. My belief and my conversation about the squirrels was creating a small box, not the squirrels. What needed to change was my belief and conversation. So I committed to change. I began to talk about how much fun they were to watch as they chased each other

through the trees. I noticed how smart they were to figure out the supposed "squirrel-proof" feeders. I began to see how they were God's little creatures that brought entertainment to my garden. Within days, I was actually rooting for them to figure out the a new bird feeder. That is when my box changed. It grew huge because I began to see the squirrels differently.

It makes me smile to think of John rooting for the squirrels. You can *"build a bigger box"* as John suggests by changing the way you talk to others and to yourself.

Ban *"can't"* from your vocabulary. Early in my childhood, I learned to approach most things from a positive point of view. I remember Mom telling me that there was no such thing as *"can't"*. She didn't even want to hear us say it.

> ## *"There is no such thing as can't."*

If you knew my mom, you would know why. At the writing of this book, she is 88 years old. She is still driving. She takes water aerobics every summer and exercises regularly the rest of the year. She even won a bathing suit contest and came in first place in a fashion show at the senior residence where she now lives.

She does not know the meaning of *"can't."* She grew up during the depression and learned how to *"stretch a dollar"* further than anyone else I know. In fact, my mother didn't start working until my younger brother, Mike, was in school, never made more than minimum wage, and still managed to save a small fortune. I didn't know this until Dad died a few years ago. I should have known. She is an amazing woman. She would say, *"Maybe you don't want to or you don't know how, but you can!"*

Since my mom used this on me, I used it on my son. From the time he was in grade school, he wanted to be in a rock band. I told him that if he really wanted it, then he could do it. I didn't want him to wake up at

40 and say, *"Gee, I wish I had."* So, I gave him a 3x5 card. He wrote his goal on it and taped it to the bathroom mirror. I guess he read it every day because when we moved from that house in 1995, that card was still there.

Guess what he is doing today? He is in a band. In fact, he is in two and sometimes three bands. He writes music, lyrics and arranges the songs. He has performed and/or produced several albums. On one, he even played all of the instruments. He and his wife, Jennifer, also book bands on tours around the country and sometimes even around the world. He is not wildly famous like the Beatles but he is doing what he loves. He is successful because he said, *"I can!"* instead of *"I can't!"*. It all came from a small phrase that I learned from my mother; *"There is no such thing as can't."*

Replace it with the positive version. Small things we say can make a difference. I can say that I want to loose twenty pounds or I can say that I want to weigh 130 pounds. These statements are both true but the second one is pointing me in the direction I want to go instead of away from what I want to avoid. If I am always thinking about how much weight I want to loose, it is very difficult, if not impossible, to think of what I want to weigh. Saying I want to weigh a certain amount gets me focused on the right thing.

It applies to everything you say. This really hit home when Trey was about 17 years old. We had been asked to give a talk at the local single parents' organization. We did some preparation beforehand. Trey and I each chose what we were going to say about each topic. We also agreed that if either one of us wanted to make a comment, we would let the other one finish and then ask for permission. I was talking about being as positive as possible with our kids, especially since they were going through some extra struggles being part of a single-parent family. When I was done, Trey asked if he could comment. Of course, I said, "Yes." I was more than a little nervous, however, about what he would say. I knew I had not been the perfect mother, and I was afraid that he might point that out.

Well, much to my surprise, he told them two things that I didn't think he even noticed while he was growing up. First, he told them that when I wanted him to do something, I said it in a positive way. For example, when I wanted to make sure he brought his jacket home from school, I would say, *"Remember your jacket,"* instead of, *"Don't forget your jacket."* I was amazed that he recognized the difference.

Catch them doing something right. Again to my surprise, he also told them about how I used to catch him doing something right and point it out. He told them about a time when he was just sitting in the living room playing with his Lincoln Logs. I walked by, tousled his hair, and said, *" You sure are a great kid."* He said that he liked that I noticed him when he was just being a "kid" instead of only noticing him when he was misbehaving. Now, he uses these techniques on *his* children.

When I worked for Fred Pryor Seminars I used to teach a class on Stress Management. I took an informal survey about what was most important to the participants about their jobs. Most managers expected them to say increased pay. While that always showed up in the top ten, it was never in the top three. Recognition was always one, two or three on the list.

> *"Catch them doing something right."*

Everyone wants to be recognized. I had a client once who told me that he paid his employees to do a great job and that he did not have to recognize his employees for doing what they were already paid to do. Technically, he was right. Getting recognized was not part of the agreement when he hired those employees. But if something so simple as recognizing someone for doing a good job will make it a better place to work, isn't it worth it? It doesn't even cost anything!

You can do it with family members, friends and even co-workers. If you are willing to start doing this on a regular basis, you will see great rewards. As John Knight says, *"Build a bigger box."*

Use "I" instead of "you". While teaching "Humans Being More Training" for Nikken, Inc. I learned the difference between using *"I"* and *"you"*. When offering your opinion or sharing your feelings it best to use *"I".* Here is how it works. Instead of saying, *"When you go to the grocery store and you're hungry, you buy too much food."* Say, *"When I go to the grocery store and I'm hungry, sometimes I buy too much food."*

Here is the difference. Now, pay attention because it is very subtle. Imagine that I have just made the first statement to you. *"When you go to the grocery store and you're hungry, you buy too much food."* You might feel a little defensive and want to say, *"I do NOT! How dare you accuse me of that!"* Now, imagine that I have said the second statement to you. *"When I go to the grocery store and I'm hungry, sometimes I buy too much food."* You are probably less likely to get defensive because I am not accusing you of anything. I am just sharing what happens to me. You might say, *"You know, that happens to me sometimes, too."* Or, *"Funny, but that has never happened to me."* It is easier for you to consider, more objectively, what I have said.

What most of us mean is *"I"* instead of *"you"* anyway. I was watching a Barbara Walters' special where she interviewed a celebrity that everyone wanted to know more about. Ms. Walters asked the actress what it was like when she didn't get a part in a movie that she really wanted. The actress replied, *"Well, when you find a really great part and you read the script and you get your heart set on getting the part…"* That is not what she meant. This was a way for her to distance herself perhaps, because she was uncomfortable about sharing her feelings. It would have been much more powerful for this actress to own her feelings. She could have said, *"When I find a really great part and I read the script, and I get my heart set on it…"* She would have come across to her audience as a strong woman who knew that she had feelings and was not afraid to admit them.

This is especially helpful when offering an opinion. People seem to respond to someone who can admit that he or she has struggled with a problem or two. Instead of saying, *"If you don't study you will flunk out of school."* Say, *"I found that when I didn't study, I really had a hard time passing. When I studied a little every night, it was much easier for me when a test came up."* Or *"If you don't get here on time you will loose your job."* Say, *"When I was in your position, one of the reasons I got promoted was because I made it a point to get here early and be at my post ready to go to work right on schedule."* People can identify with you more easily if you are not lecturing them.

Next time you share an opinion or feeling, notice whether you use *"I"* or *"you."* If you are sharing a feeling or opinion use *"I"*. It is simple way for you to own your feelings. You will come from a position of strength instead of weakness. Strong people own their feelings.

Use "You're right" instead of "I know". Here is another small phrase that can make a big difference in your dialogue with others. Think of the last time that someone told you something that you did not want to hear. You knew it was right; you just didn't want to hear it. For example, you have a slight kidney infection and mom says, *"You should drink more water."* What do you say in response? If you are like me, you probably said, *"I know, I know."* Which is true! My question is, *"If you knew, then how come you didn't do it?"* What would happen if you said, *"You're right,"* instead? Again, there is a profound but subtle difference.

Consider how your mom felt when you said, *"I know, I know."* Consider how she would have felt if you had said, *"You're right."* For you, it might not make much difference. You are admitting that your mom is right, either way. For your mom it might be very different. She would probably feel more valuable. And in spite of what you might think, you will probably feel better, too. *"I know"* is much more defensive than *"You're right."* Agreeing with someone when you know that she is right is always better than defensiveness.

Have a change of heart. I heard someone say recently, *"I had a change of heart."* It made me think that our conversation is a result of what is in our heart. Take a close look at the words you use. It might be rather frightening to admit that the words that come from your mouth are in your heart. The good news is that you can have a change of heart. You have a choice.

If you make the effort to change your language, you will benefit from that effort and so will everyone around you. Make sure you are playing the right internal tapes. Encourage yourself the way you encourage others. Ban *"can't "* from your vocabulary. Choose positive language. Catch people doing something right. Use *"I"* instead of *"you"* when sharing your feelings. When you agree with someone say, *"You're right."* instead of *"I know."* While this is a long list and each one may seem small and insignificant, watch what happens once you make them a habit.

Suggestion for action this week:

1.   Make a list of the negative things you say to yourself.
2.   Change these into positive statements.
3.   Write the positive statements on a 3x5 card and put it in your wallet or purse.
4.   Read the statements aloud at least twice a day.
5.   Make a tape of your new self-talk.
6.   Whenever you hear yourself playing the old tape, stop and turn it around, out loud if possible.
7.   Make a list of some of the things you say that you would like to change.
8.   Choose one to work on this week.
9.   Enlist someone to help you keep track of how often you use the word or phrase.
10. Write out some things you could say instead.
11. Set up a way to talk with your buddy/coach at least once a week to give him/her a progress report.

WEEK FOUR

Gentlemen (and Ladies), Start Your Engines

I am not much of a racing fan, but I have watched the start of the Daytona 500 a few times. There is always so much excitement when the announcer says, *"Gentlemen, start your engines!"* Even when watching on television I can feel the anticipation of the crowd. If we all approached life with the enthusiasm of the racecar drivers, it would certainly be more exciting. In this chapter you will learn how important it is to embrace life.

What happens when you say "no" and you mean "yes"?

I know someone who always says, *"no."* Even if he doesn't say it out loud, his first reaction to every suggestion is no. He lives in fear of what someone will corner him into doing. He has missed out on so many things because of his tendency to say no. It is much more rewarding to say yes to life.

William Glasser, well-known author of *Reality Therapy*, spoke to my school district when I was a teacher. He said, *"Don't say 'no' when you really mean 'yes'."* There are times when it is wise to say *"no"*. However, it is important to determine the difference.

> *"Don't say 'no', when you really mean 'yes'!"*
> *William Glasser*

I used to have a friend who automatically turned down every invitation. It happened so often that it became a habit. Eventually, she would agree to come to a party or have lunch, but not until we had begged and pleaded with her to come. Somehow, we all knew that she really wanted to go. Maybe her way of feeling good about herself was to be begged and cajoled. We eventually gave up asking her. It was just too much work to get her to go anywhere with us.

This is a great lesson to teach children. Paul has always employed this technique when dealing with his kids. If we were going somewhere, he would ask them once if they wanted to go. If they said *"no"*, then he left them behind. I always wanted to talk them into coming. But he was right. After missing out a couple of times, they both learned to be honest and tell us what they really wanted.

Pay attention to your answers. Don't say *"no"* when you really mean *"yes"*. You might miss something very rewarding. Even if it isn't rewarding, at least you learned something new. Rejecting something that you explored is better than rejecting something you know nothing about.

What happens when you look for opportunities to grow?

Another way to say *"yes"* to life is to look for opportunities to grow. My friend Doug gave me this story. It is a great example of someone who said *"yes"* to life.

> On the first day of school, our professor introduced himself and challenged us to get to know someone we didn't already know. I stood up to look around, when a gentle hand touched my shoulder. I turned around to find a wrinkled, little old lady beaming up at me with a smile that lit up her entire being.

She said, "Hi, handsome. My name is Rose. I'm eighty-seven years old. Can I give you a hug?" I laughed and enthusiastically responded, "Of course you may!" And she gave me a giant squeeze.

"Why are you in college at such a young, innocent age?" I asked. She jokingly replied, "I'm here to meet a rich husband, get married, have a couple of children, and then retire and travel."

"No, seriously," I asked. I was curious what may have motivated her to be taking on this challenge at her age. "I always dreamed of having a college education and now I'm getting one!" she told me. After class we walked to the student union building and shared a chocolate milkshake. We became instant friends. Every day for the next three months we would leave class together and talk nonstop. I was always mesmerized listening to this "time machine" as she shared her wisdom and experience with me.

Over the course of the year, Rose became a campus icon as she easily made friends wherever she went. She loved to dress up and she reveled in the attention bestowed upon her from the other students. She was living it up.

At the end of the semester, we invited Rose to speak at our football banquet. I'll never forget what she taught us. She was introduced and stepped up to the podium. As she began to deliver her prepared speech, she dropped her three-by-five cards on the floor. Frustrated and a little embarrassed, she leaned into the microphone and simply said, "I'm sorry I'm so jittery. I gave up beer for Lent and this whiskey is killing me! I'll never get my speech back in order so let me just tell you what I know."

As we laughed she cleared her throat and began: "We do not stop playing because we are old; we grow old because we stop playing. There are only four secrets to staying young, being happy and achieving success. You have to laugh and find humor every day.

"You've got to have a dream. When you lose your dreams, you die. We have so many people walking around who are dead and don't even know it!

"There is a huge difference between growing older and growing up. If you are nineteen years old and lie in bed for one full year and don't do one productive thing, you will turn twenty years old. If I am eighty-seven years old and stay in bed for a year and never do anything I will turn eighty-eight. Anybody can grow older. That doesn't take any talent or ability. The idea is to grow up by always finding the opportunity in change.

"Have no regrets. The elderly usually don't have regrets for what we did, but rather for things we did not do. The only people who fear death are those with regrets." She concluded her speech by courageously singing "The Rose." She challenged each of us to study the lyrics and live them out in our daily lives. At the year's end, Rose finished the college degree she had begun all those years ago. One week after graduation Rose died peacefully in her sleep. Over two thousand college students attended her funeral in tribute to the wonderful woman who taught by example that it's never too late to be all you can possibly be.

Remember that growing older is mandatory, but growing up is optional.

That is a great story! Lots of people would have understood if Rose had not finished college at her age. Rose wanted to have a productive life. She did not use the excuse that she was too old.

> *"Growing older is mandatory, but growing up is optional."*

I want to be like Rose. I want to live to be 104 years old! The operative word here is *"live."* I don't want to simply exist until I am 104. I don't want to be on life support. I want to exercise and travel and give speeches and write books and have fun…all the way to the end. You can do that too by looking for opportunities to grow.

What happens when you take a risk?

Enlightened Leadership by Ed Oakley and Doug Krug states that 80% of people in the world are Reactive Thinkers and 20% are Creative Thinkers. Their book was written specifically to help managers deal with these two types of employees in business. It can also help us make a choice in the way we approach things.

As you can imagine, the Creative Thinkers are the people who accomplish the most. They are open to change, build on successes, take responsibility for their actions, and are willing to take risks. Reactive Thinkers are resistant to change, blinded by the problems in the situation, devastated by failure, place blame, and avoid responsibility. You can see that Creative Thinkers say *"yes"* to life and Reactive Thinkers don't.

You will never learn anything new if you always play it safe. For example, I will never be a great snow skier because I am afraid to take risks on the slopes. My stepdaughter, Anna, on the other hand, will risk almost anything just to see what happens.

When she was about eight years old, she and her brother Chris came to visit us from Louisiana. It was during the winter and they had never seen snow. Paul and I took them skiing. Of course, we started on the bunny hill. In no time flat, Anna was on the intermediate hills alone going faster than I was. And I had been skiing for years. She was willing to take the risk, and I wasn't. Of course, her brother was not far behind her. There was no way that he was going to let Anna outdo him. They both became much better at skiing that year than I will ever be because they were willing to take a chance.

What do you learn when you make a mistake?

Don't be afraid of making a mistake. I would never hire anyone who said that they had never made a mistake. I would know that they were either lying or had never risked anything.

There is a story about a junior executive that worked for a very large computer company. He made a very expensive mistake. After he realized his mistake, he went back to his office and began packing his belongings in a box, planning to leave his resignation letter on his boss' desk on the way out. As he was packing, the boss walked by and stopped to ask the young man what he was doing. *"Why, packing my things, of course. Didn't you hear what I did today?"*

"Of course I heard!" said the boss.

"Well, I thought I would save you the trouble of firing me."

"What do you mean fire you? We just spent ten thousand dollars on your education. Do you think you will ever make that mistake again? No! But your replacement might. Unpack that box and get back to work. We need to fix this problem and you are the one who needs to fix it!"

By saying *"yes"* instead of *"no"*, looking for opportunities to grow, taking an educated risk occasionally and by learning from your mistakes, you might just find some new and exciting things you enjoy. Go for it! You deserve it!

Suggestions for action this week:

1. Count the number of times you say or think *"no"* when offered an opportunity. Write in your journal about this experience.

2. Answer this question in your journal: What have I said "no" to that I wish I had said "yes" to in my past?
3. Make a list of things you missed out on because you did not say "yes". Keep it in your journal and add to it regularly.
4. Take a risk this week and write about it in your journal.
5. Write about a time when you made a mistake and what you learned.

WEEK FIVE

Own that Driver's Seat

When I learned to drive it gave me a real sense of power. I could go anywhere I wanted at any time I wanted…provided my parents gave me the keys to the car. The difference, now, is that I can own that driver's seat if I am willing to overcome defeat. I get to choose how I react to everything life gives me. In this chapter, you will see how overcoming defeat, instead of being overwhelmed by it, will put *you* in that diver's seat.

What can you do to shape your future?

Do you remember the now classic ad for the Winter Olympics called "The Thrill of Victory…The Agony of Defeat"? I still cringe when I see that tragic fall. In contrast, you only have to experience agony if you let defeat overwhelm you…if you let it stop you.

Acknowledge your past. Gail Majcher is a dynamic woman I have come to know over the past five years. Gail has written a book, *A Worthy Woman,* in the hopes that other women will choose to overcome defeat, instead of being overwhelmed by defeat.

> *"You can choose to overcome defeat instead of being overwhelmed by defeat."*

Gail was a victim of domestic violence. After being brutally battered for four years, she escaped the marriage with two babies, no education, no money and few people to help her. She had to go on welfare as she struggled to turn her life around. Unlike so many others, she survived with her children and made a success of her life in spite of the emotional scars. She chose to say, *"Yes, I have been abused and battered, and I choose to make something of my life. No one will ever abuse my children or me again. And, I choose to use this experience to help others with the same challenges."*

Find the courage to move on. Today she has a Ph.D. in Psychology and has a well-established private practice. She is married to a wonderful man who honors and cherishes her. He encourages her to continue to help others. He has even worked with her on fundraising for a local shelter for battered women.

I teach a weekend seminar for Nikken, Inc. called "Humans Being More". At one point, we explore the possibility that things in your past may be holding you back from moving forward. One day, a participant came up to me after the seminar and told me about what she discovered. She asked me not to share it during that seminar but gave me permission to share it later if I thought it would help someone.

A close family member had sexually molested her as a child. Until now, she had not been able to even talk about it. During the exercise, she was able to let go of the anger she had been carrying around for years. She was able to forgive the perpetrator. She does not condone his behavior, of course, but during the exercise she realized that holding onto the bitterness and anger was keeping her from growing while having absolutely no impact on him at all. She let go so she could improve her life. She now thinks of him with pity, not hate. She had not been able to do that before. She changed her perspective.

These are tragic situations. I am not sure I could have done what Gail or this young woman did, but I admire them for moving on. I hope that whatever you are dealing with is not so serious. Whatever it is, acknowledge it, and find the courage to move on. They both found more courage than they ever believed possible. They found something besides bitterness and anger. You can, too.

What can you do for support?

Find a Cheerleader. Sometimes you may need some encouragement to overcome your past. I have had some great cheerleaders in my life. Every one of them has helped keep me from becoming a victim at one time or another. For example, I have met for breakfast on a regular basis for almost twenty years with my friends, Karen and JoAnn. At first, we met every week. We would each spend time sharing our goals and telling each other what kind of help we needed. Sometimes we had a suggestion; sometimes we just offered a willing ear or a shoulder to cry on.

I remember one time in particular when Karen, JoAnn and I were still all attending *Single Pointe*, a large singles organizations in the Detroit area. Karen was dating a guy that she thought was *"the one"*. He broke up with her and started dating someone else right away. Karen was devastated. She could hardly talk about it without crying. JoAnn and I agreed to pray for her and just be there for her. I remember saying something like; *"Someday you will be thankful for this."*

JoAnn and I began to thank God for this situation. I wasn't even sure why, but I just knew that it would all work out. Of course, Karen couldn't see that at the time. Today she is very thankful. She is married to a great guy who has two wonderful kids. Those kids are now married and each have one child that call Karen *"Grandma"*.

We have seen each other through many relationships, deaths in our families, major moves, and job changes. It is so nice not to have to start from scratch when telling a story. We know each other's weaknesses, yet we remain each other's cheerleaders.

Sometimes we have to speak out when we see each other screw up. For example, once I was dating a *"loser"* in more ways than one. My friends never stopped loving me, but they never let me make excuses about him. I finally stopped seeing him, yet they never threw it up to me or tried to make me feel foolish for having dated him in the first place.

Now, we meet less than once a month because of our busy schedules. We don't spend as much time talking about our goals anymore. Most of the time is spent just catching up, but we are still the best of friends. We have seen each other through some of the toughest times in our lives.

We have confronted and comforted. We have laughed and we have cried. And we have prayed…oh, how we have prayed! We have even been so broke that we couldn't exchange gifts at Christmas. And no matter where life leads us, there will always be a bond because of what we have been through together. Karen and JoAnn know things about me that even my husband doesn't know. Yet they love me still!

Jan Schleicher is a business coach. We met when I was doing some training at General Motors, where she worked at the time. In spite of the fact that we have both changed jobs and she moved to northern Michigan, we have stayed in touch.

One day at lunch, I shared with Jan that I wanted to get better at keeping up my Bible study. God was a priority for a long time but I always found other things to do instead (like work on this book!) Jan offered to be my accountability partner. She suggested that I call her each week. I would tell her how many times during the week I had taken time to pray, read the Bible or spend time with God. She never nagged me or put me down. She was patient and encouraging. That is what I needed. Before long, I was back on track with my Bible study and prayer. We still talk about once a week.

Be a Cheerleader. A few years ago, one of my clients invited me to attend a class he was offering to his employees. The instructor was Gary LaLonde. During the eight-week class, we were to pair up with someone and become each other's encourager. Every day we were to ask each other, *"What can I do for you today?"*

I did this for about three months with my partner, Susan Linan. It felt good both to be the giver and the receiver. It was nice to know that she cared about what was going on in my life and would take the time to listen. On some days, neither of us had a need, but just knowing that someone was there ready to help was so comforting. I was looking for some additional training jobs and Susan referred me to some people she knew that needed some training. She was looking for a job and I listened to each opportunity and gave her some input. We helped each other.

Sometimes when I am being a cheerleader, I can forget what is troubling me. If you don't have any friends or family members who need support, find an organization that helps the less fortunate, and volunteer. I have done some work with single mothers. Since I was a single mom for almost twelve years, it seems to mean something to them. I have been there. I survived. Perhaps that gives them the hope they need to believe that they can do it too.

Being someone's cheerleader is a great way to find a cheerleader. I have another friend, Carol. She is such a good friend that I could tell her she was making a big mistake when, in 1989, she was going to break up with someone that she was dating because he was *"too nice."* I sat her down and had a heart-to-heart talk with her. I suggested that the reason she didn't like him was because she was only used to men who treated her badly. Well, she reconsidered and now they have been married for ten years.

I was Carol's cheerleader then and she is mine now. She is always so excited for me when I accomplish something new. She always acts like I am so amazing to her. I feel special when I am with her. We even share the same birthday. Last year she gave me a picture frame that said, "Friends Forever." It sits prominently on my dresser with a picture of us inside. She was even there for me when we had to put our dog, Tiffy, to sleep because she was dying from breast cancer. She listened and even shed a tear with me. Everyone needs a cheerleader from time to time.

Consider hiring a coach. I used a personal fitness coach named Johannes Arnold who helped me get in shape physically. We only worked on that one area of my life. He was a personal trainer working for a company called Lifetime Fitness. We worked together for about six months twice a week. He got me to lift weights for the first time in my life.

I lost almost twenty pounds and gained a great deal of stamina. I used to get out of breath if I had to run to catch a plane. After working with him just a few weeks, I could walk up a flight of stairs and not even get winded. My clothes fit better and I felt great. Until I began working with Johannes, there was no one there to tell me I was doing a great job or to encourage me to work a little harder. After working with him for six months, he set up an exercise regimen for me to follow.

When I was preparing to become a coach, I hired a Personal Business Coach, Barry Demp. Barry was good at getting me to stretch my thinking. He pushed me to excel. He is one of the few people I know that can get me out of my comfort zone. He wouldn't let me give up on myself. I don't talk to him every week anymore but I know he is there for me when I need him.

What is your next step?

Once you have acknowledged your past, decided to move on and found some support, you are ready to take the next step. Because you own that drivers seat, the choice is up to you.

Be a Survivor. Unlike the popular reality television show, you don't get voted out of life. It is a choice. You get to be a survivor by making a choice not by making it through another tally of the votes. The key is to vow to never be a victim again. You can be like the fictional character in "Gone with the Wind", Scarlet O'Hara, who said, *"As God is my witness, I will never go hungry again."* Look at your challenge and begin to see it as a catalyst for change.

> *"Look at your challenge as a catalyst for change."*

A number of years ago, John Stossel from ABC news did a special called *"The Blame Game"* about the victimization of America. He explored the ways our society has become a culture of victims. Everybody's got some serious problem that was caused by somebody else! Some, I am sure, are quite serious. On the other hand, it seems that if people don't want to take responsibility for their behavior, they create a syndrome. There is even a syndrome for people who are habitually late. John Stossel now has a regular feature on 20/20 called "Give me a break!" That is what I want to say when I hear about a syndrome for people who are habitually late. *"Give me a break."* Or, as my stepdaughter, Anna is so fond of saying, *"Get a life!"*

Most people who are habitually late are just making bad choices. I have been there. Before I met my husband, Paul, I was always late. I was one of those people whose friends told them 7:00 if it was really 7:30 so that they wouldn't have to wait for me. I claimed to have tried everything. Then one day, I was on the way to a meeting. I was running late because I did not give myself enough time to get there. I began to hope that there was a traffic jam on the freeway so I could blame the traffic for my tardiness. "Give me a break!" It was 5:00. I knew that. If I had planned better, then I would have given myself more time to get somewhere in rush hour.

Be grateful for your challenges. Mike Wickett is a professional speaker who has published some tapes with Nightingale Conant. I took his *Growth through Goals* class back in 1980 and ended up working for him. In one session, he asked us to write down what we were grateful for. I began by writing the usual things like my son, my home, my country. He was walking around the class just talking while people were writing. He was making suggestions and I could see people mentally say, *"Yes, I like that one,"* and write it down. Then he asked a very curious question. *"Can you be thankful for someone who has done something terrible to you?"*

I immediately thought of my second husband. He left me for another woman after I had left my first husband for him. How could I ever be thankful for him? Then, I began to think. If it hadn't been for my ex-husband I would not be in Michigan—which I love. If it had not been for my ex-husband, I would never have quit smoking. He found Smokenders in the newspaper. I decided to say "Yes and…" that day and I have been looking for ways to say it ever since.

It has not always been easy. There are times I have wanted to give up. Like most everyone, when things went wrong, I wanted to wallow in self-pity. It would have been so much easier. Self-pity is like an old sweatsuit. It is so comfortable and easy to wear. I could just curl up and go to sleep feeling sorry for myself. Then I remembered the frog in the water that slowly began to boil him alive and I sat up and said, *"NO! I will not go there. Been there, done that. It doesn't work."* All the pain is worth it if you learn from it. It is only a waste if you let it bury you in guilt or shame.

What is the best dialogue?

It is time to take responsibility for who you are today, despite the hardships of your past. The way you talk about your past will have an impact on how much affect it has on your future.

Use "yes, and…" instead of "yes, but…". Think of the young woman I mentioned earlier that was molested as a child. If anyone has a valid reason to feel like a victim, she does. She could say, *"Yes, but I was molested as a child."* However, she chose to say, *"Yes, I was molested as a child, and I can learn from that and move on."* Even people who were drug addicts or alcoholics often go on to help other people, once they recover themselves. We do not have to remain a victim.

I have told you about my two divorces. There are people in this world that would allow me to be bitter and angry. They might even agree with me if I said I was a failure. I am neither rich nor famous, so some people might not think of me as successful, but I have chosen a *"Yes, and..."* attitude.

> *"The way you talk about your past will have an impact on how much affect it has on your future."*

I have volunteered at the *Divorce Recovery Class* to be a small group leader. My husband and I have taught *Rethinking Marriage while Thinking Remarriage* for people about to embark on a second or even a third marriage. My choice was to say," <u>Yes</u>, *I have been divorced. I left my first husband. My second husband left me.* <u>And</u>, *I choose to learn from those experiences. I choose to help others grow."* Like others who broke the four-minute mile after Roger Bannister did, maybe you can use these experiences to help you realize that you are also capable of choosing *"Yes, and..."*

Here is an example of how it might work for you. You can replace any challenge for the one I have chosen.

My challenge:

I am 50 pounds overweight.

The advice I have heard:

Eat better. Start exercising. Take some healthy supplements.

My past reaction:

<u>Yes, but</u>...I have been this way for so long I can't help it. Or,
<u>Yes, but</u>...<u>I</u> have tried before and it didn't work for me. Or,
<u>Yes, but</u>...everyone in my family is overweight; I will never be slim.

The new reaction that I choose:

<u>Yes, and</u>...I like myself this way. I am learning to love myself just the way I am, and I refuse to buy into the Madison Avenue picture of who I should be. Or,

<u>Yes, and</u>…I am done making excuses; I am not going to let anything stand in my way this time. Or,

<u>Yes, and</u>…I need help and I am not ashamed to ask for it.

Do you have a problem that has been harassing you for years? Maybe it just started a few days ago. When you hear some good advice, do you want to say, *"<u>Yes</u>, <u>but</u> you don't know what it is like"*? Or, *"<u>Yes</u>, <u>but</u> I am too old or too young or too anything"*? Stop right now and say, *"<u>Yes</u>, <u>and</u> you know what I have learned?"* It may take some time at first. Use this process for every *"Yes, but"* statement you find yourself using. In spite of how hard this may be, it has the potential to make a huge impact on your life.

Use "Challenge" instead of "Problem" The next thing you can do is replace the word problem with challenge. A problem seems so overwhelming. A challenge is something you can face with resolve. If you say challenge instead of problem, it may create a very different image for you. You will begin to see yourself meeting this challenge and overcoming it.

Perhaps you have heard the story of David and Goliath. David was a small shepherd boy. He was sent on an errand and ended up killing a Philistine giant. Maybe your *"challenge"* is overwhelming, like David's. Perhaps you have worn the comfortable sweatsuit of self-pity long enough. Now is the time to take off the sweatsuit and get your slingshot out and kill that giant that has been harassing you for so many years.

Acknowledge your past and shape your future. Find support from others during your journey. Talk about where you are going, not just where you have been. Remember that because you own that driver's seat, you get to choose where you want to go.

Suggestions for Action this week:

1. Write down one thing that you want to change.
2. Write the "Yes, but…" statement/s you have been using.

3. Write a new "Yes, and…" statement for each one of the "Yes, but…"statements.
4. Share these with a friend.
5. Ask him/her to hold you accountable.

Week Six

Conquer the Roadblocks

I have had more than my share of roadblocks. Conquering them has been a challenge as well as a great learning experience. Every time I make it through another one I gain more confidence and skill. Conquering the roadblocks in your life will give you more confidence and skill as well. You will learn how to overcome the defeats in your life that might have held you back in the past.

When I moved to Michigan, I had been teaching for five years. While I was very comfortable standing in front of my class of elementary students, I had not done much speaking in front of adults. One day the principle asked me to do a demonstration in front of the staff about a technique that I was using with my students. I can still remember how nervous I was. I am sure you could hear my knees knocking in the back of the room. I decided that day to get comfortable with public speaking. I had no idea that some day I would make a living speaking with one of the largest public training companies in the nation presenting to audiences from forty to four hundred.

Perhaps you, like many others, have a fear of public speaking. In 1981, I took the Dale Carnegie Sales Course. This course builds confidence in salespeople by getting them up to make a presentation several times during each class. Facing a fear is a great way to take away its power.

What do you see when you look in the mirror?

Facing your fears might be one of the hardest things you will ever do. Are you willing to look in the mirror right now? Are you willing to take a really hard look and face your fears? If you are, then here are some fears that I have found in some of the bravest people I know. In fact, the very act of looking in the mirror is a very brave thing to do.

Financial

♦ Being broke
♦ Being poor
♦ Not having enough money to pay the bills
♦ Loosing money in the stock market
♦ Never having enough in savings

Professional

♦ Loosing my job
♦ Not getting a raise
♦ Not getting a promotion
♦ Not being the best
♦ Being demoted

Physical

♦ Gaining weight
♦ Getting a life threatening disease
♦ Being in constant pain
♦ Loosing the use of my limbs
♦ Loosing my eyesight

Recreational

♦ Never having any fun
♦ Not being able to take a vacation

- Not being able to read or watch my favorite shows
- Not being able to play my favorite sport
- Not being able to relax

Emotional

- Not believing in myself
- Never experiencing joy
- Succumbing to the pressures of life
- Being depressed most of the time
- Being afraid to venture out

Mental

- Loosing my capacity to reason
- Never having the opportunity to increase my skills
- Loosing interest in gaining knowledge
- Becoming mentally stagnant
- Not being able to exchange ideas with others intellectually

Spiritual

- Loosing my faith in God
- Becoming skeptical of everything I can't see
- Loosing my capacity to pray
- Not being able to share my spiritual beliefs openly
- Being persecuted for my beliefs

Relational

- Growing old alone
- Not being able to count on anyone for support
- Not having a good relationship with my family members
- Not having any friends
- Never getting to know my grandchildren

General

♦ Fear of success
♦ Fear of failure
♦ Fear of public speaking
♦ Fear of high places
♦ Fear of being out in public
♦ Fear of tight spaces
♦ Fear of flying
♦ Fear of death
♦ Fear of _____

The most important question you can ask yourself this week is "What am I afraid of and what am I going to do about it?" Some of your fears may not be wise to face. That young lady who was molested as a child does not need to face the perpetrator. Coming to that conclusion is the best step you can take. For other less serious fears, make a decision to face them and follow through. Remember: *Most people will not change until it is more uncomfortable to be where they are than it is to get where they want to go.*

Look at four stages of change again: Unconscious Incompetent, Conscious Incompetent, Conscious Competent, and Unconscious Competent. Now that you have read about these fears you cannot be unconscious any longer. If you are uncomfortable enough to move forward, you are now in the Conscious Incompetent Stage. It takes a very *brave* person to move into the Conscious Competent Stage. And it takes a very *persistent* person to move into the Unconscious Competent Stage.

What does it mean to be brave?

Brave means to have or show courage under difficult or dangerous conditions. It does not mean that someone has no fear. If there were no fear, no one would have to be brave. Zig Ziglar says that fear stands for false evidence appearing real.

> *"It takes a brave person to move into the*
> *Conscious Competent Stage."*

You can use the following process with any fear.

First, ask, "What is the worst that could happen?" Talk to others who have faced your fear and won. You can approach people you know if you are sure that they will be supportive. There are organizations where people gather to discuss a fear. There are also therapists that specialize in overcoming fears.

Second, learn everything you can about what your fear. Find the best resources available. Take a class or read a book. In the case of public speaking, learn everything you can about the mechanics of making a presentation. Dale Carnegie is a great place to do that.

Third, be prepared. Have a plan in place to implement when necessary. Make it a solid plan that you are confident will work if something happens and you are confronted with having to deal with your fear. When you are prepared, you will not live in dread of what might happen.

Being brave means that you have courage to take the steps you need to overcome a difficult situation. Learn everything you can about your fear. Talk to others who have been where you are today and moved beyond. Have a contingency plan in place that will be a safety valve for you. You will still be Conscious Competent at this point. The next steps will take you to Unconscious Competent.

What can you do to exhibit persistence?

Newt Rockney once said, "*When the going gets tough, the tough get going.*" But I believe that when the going gets tough, most people quit. Don't quit now. You are almost there.

First, find a safe place. You need an opportunity to address your fear that is both safe and accessible. It needs to be accessible so you won't have an excuse not to do what you set out to do. It needs to be safe so you don't have to add another fear to the mix. For instance, if the place you need to go is in another state and in an unsafe neighborhood, you will probably not go very often.

> *"It takes a very persistent person to move into the Unconscious Competent Stage."*

For instance, joining Toastmasters might be just the right place for you to practice a presentation without feeling self-conscious. Everyone there is an amateur. It is also easy to access in most areas because there are chapter in many locations. If there is not a chapter near you then start one.

Second, practice every chance you get. If you remember learning to ride a bike, you will see how important practice is. You may have had a few skinned knees but you kept it up until you became Unconscious Competent. Public speaking in no different. In order to get past your fear, you need to give more speeches.

I remember my first speech. I was so nervous that I had to hold on to the podium so my hands would stop shaking. Now I can get up and give a spontaneous talk on just about any topic that I am familiar with and not miss a beat. This happened, not because of any great ability, but because of the hundreds of free talks I gave for anyone willing to listen. Lots of practice in a safe and accessible environment is the key to overcoming your fear.

Now that you have looked in the mirror and faced your fears you are half way to becoming Unconscious Competent. All that is necessary now is to be brave and be persistent.

Suggestions for Action this week:

1. Make a list of your fears.
2. Ask "What is the worst that can happen?" Answer this question in your journal.

3. Make a list of things you missed out on because were afraid. Keep it in your journal and add to it regularly.
4. Take one step toward facing a fear this week. Write about the experience in your journal.

WEEK SEVEN

Enjoy the Ride

I used to have to drive about forty miles in rush hour traffic twice a day because I worked in the city and lived in the suburbs. It was a grueling drive in the snow. I had a hard time learning to enjoy the ride. Someone suggested that I turn my car into a university on wheels. Once I did, it made the whole ride much more rewarding. Once you choose joy over happiness, it will make *every* experience in your life more rewarding. This week, you will learn why.

What makes you happy?

In my quest to understand change, one area was particularly troubling for me. It was the difference between joy and happiness. The root word for happiness is *hap* (Middle English, 1100-1500 AD). This is also the root for happen or happening, as in an event. Since happiness and happening come from the same root word then happiness and happening are related. It seems to me that happiness occurs for a specific time because of an event or happening.

For instance, I was not very happy when Trey and his family moved from Michigan to Washington in January 2000. However, I was very happy in May of that same year when Angela and Chris, my stepson, got married. My level of happiness at that moment was based on a particular event. Because I was *unhappy* about the event in January and then *happy* about the event in May, does that mean that I was unhappy between these two events? Or, does it mean that I remained *happy* from May 2000 until another event occurred that made me *unhappy*? I hope not!

Events don't make you happy. Everyday we experience events that we like, and some that we don't. If our feelings were only dependent on what events occurred each day, then we'd be on a constant roller coaster ride. While you may enjoy a roller coaster ride from time to time, imagine living on one 24/7.

People don't make you happy. Another thing that I discovered was that most of us expect other people to make us happy. While I was married to my first husband, we were seeing a marriage counselor. She asked me a question. *"Does your happiness depend on how your husband feels at any given moment?"* I was shocked to realize that it did, and that was part of our problem. I expected *him* to make me happy.

Even though I learned that lesson well, like many people who learn a new lesson, I reacted like a pendulum and swung too far in the opposite direction. I began to only care about me. Although I professed to care about my son, I was selfish and left a good marriage for another man I didn't even know, I took my son with me an moved over a thousand miles from his father.

> ## *"Happiness is fleeting."*

Did that bring me happiness? Perhaps for a time. But within five years, I was divorced again and *"looking for love in all the wrong places."* I spent the next eight years looking for events to make me happy. I learned in counseling with my first husband that another person cannot make me happy. During my second marriage and subsequent divorce, I learned that events can't make me happy either.

What is the difference between joy and happiness?

By 1981 I had recovered from my second divorce. I had a promising job selling Growth Through Goals for Mike Wickett and I was teaching SmokEnders. I was making new friends and my son was attending a great prep school. The events and people where all in place. I had everything I wanted, but I was still not happy.

I can remember saying that my life was like a jigsaw puzzle. There were a few cracks but for the most part it was put together skillfully with a lot of hard work on my part. The only problem was that there was one piece missing right in the middle of the blue sky. I couldn't find it anywhere. I tried to put other things in its place (career, business, partying) but nothing really fit.

Doing *"my own thing"*, like everyone else in the 70's, didn't teach me the real lesson that I needed to learn. It wasn't until 1981 that I learned that I had to choose joy over happiness. Happiness is fleeting, but joy lasts a lifetime.

I was taking the Dale Carnegie Sales Course. Because I won the sales talk semi finals, I went out after class to celebrate with some other students. We were in a popular gathering place and I heard one of the graduate assistants, Jim, talking about God to another class member. I remember thinking, *"What a strange thing to be talking about in a bar."* Then I heard something that had a profound affect on me.

"God loves us so much that He gave His Son to pay the penalty for our sins." He said it was like a judge convicting me of a crime and then paying the fine for me. I found that hard to believe. After all, I had made some pretty big mistakes in my life. I had always known that Jesus had died on the cross for my sins but I thought I still had to pay for those sins again. What I came to understand that night was that while I was still messing up my life, God loved me. I also learned that he would continue to love me no matter what happened.

In the dictionary, joy is defined as feelings of great happiness or pleasure, especially of an elevated or spiritual kind. On the way home that night, I experienced that kind of joy. I asked God to forgive me for all the things I had done. I told Him that I wanted to experience the joy that Jim talked about. I began to cry. When I was done, I felt renewed.

Now the jigsaw puzzle is complete. I can still see the lines between the pieces. Every once in a while, something or someone bumps the table and things get a little messed up. Some of the pieces have even fallen on the floor. The difference now is that *God* puts them back. And for some reason, when He puts them back, they fit better. I can hardly see the lines any more. And no matter what happens, I have the joy that comes from knowing that I am loved unconditionally by God.

What's the worst that can happen?

When Trey was about nine years old, he learned about the difference between happiness and joy, too. When I would get upset during those rough years of being a single parent, Trey would ask me, *"What is the worst that can happen?"* It always helped put things in perspective.

One particular time I remember well. We were living in a condo and didn't have much money. I was doing the laundry and, when I went into the basement to put the clothes in the dryer, I discovered that the washer had overflowed. I started crying and screaming. I didn't know what I was going to do. I didn't have the money to get the washing machine fixed, and I didn't know how to fix it.

Trey heard the commotion and came down the stairs, sloshed through the water and said, *"What's wrong? Do you need a hug?"* Then he put his arm around me and looked up at me with those big brown eyes of his and said, *"Come on, Mom. What's the worst that could happen?"* It still brings tears to my eyes to think of that. I had so much to be thankful for and here I was lamenting over an overflowing washer. At least it was in the basement where there was a drain. As it turned out, there was something small stuck in the hose. I didn't even have to call a repair service to fix it.

"Joy lasts for a lifetime!"

Joy is a choice. For me, joy is no longer dependent on an event or a person. Joy is a choice. I can even be joyful in the midst of an unhappy event. When Trey and Jennifer moved to Seattle, that was an unhappy event for Paul and me, but a happy one for them. My joy comes from the fact that they love each other and their children. My joy comes from the fact that they want us to visit and they want to visit us. My joy comes from the fact that Jennifer shows August and Hazel our pictures every day so they will know who we are.

I can even have joy in the midst to tears. I can have joy when I choose to look at the good and not just the bad. It is not always an easy choice, but it is simple. Sometimes I have to consciously choose to experience joy. I am not in that Unconscious Competent Stage yet. But every day that I choose joy over happiness, I get closer.

My husband gave me a copy of saying that is on the door of our fridge. It says: *"This is God. I will be handling all of your problems today. I will not need your help, so have a good day."* It has been there for so long that sometimes I forget to read it. But when I do, it reminds me of how much I have to be grateful for.

Be grateful. I have a friend, Sadie Bolos, who speaks about attitude. Sadie tells a story about one woman who said that she hated her job. Sadie asked her if she got paid. *"Of course"*, she said.

"Well, would you rather work somewhere where you don't get paid?"

"Of course not."

"Well, write it down as something you love and appreciate about your job." Once Sadie was done with her, she had fifty things that she appreciated about her job.

A month later the woman called and said, *"Sadie, the people at work have really changed!"* Who really changed? Not the people at work but the woman who found some things to be grateful for. She found the joy. You can do the same thing.

During Week One, you took inventory in eight categories. Look at that list again.

- Financial
- Professional
- Physical
- Recreational
- Mental
- Emotional
- Spiritual
- Relational

Think of five things that you are grateful for in each category. Write them in your journal. I found that after doing this exercise, I have more joy in my life, no matter what is happening at the time.

Recognize the times you allow people to steal your joy. Notice the events that keep you from feeling joy. Ask, "What's the worst that can happen?" Be grateful for something everyday. You will begin to experience joy even in the midst of sorrow.

Suggestions for Action this week:

1. Write down the things that you are grateful for on a 3x5 card or small sheet of paper.
2. Put it in your wallet. Put a copy on your refrigerator. Put one on your bathroom mirror. Look at them often.
3. Make a journal entry every time you let an event or person steal your joy.
4. Make a journal entry every time you notice yourself feeling joy in your life.
5. Write about something that brings you joy each day this week in your journal. (If you follow this thirteen-week process, at the end

of the year you will have a list of twenty-eight things that bring you joy.)

6.   When you are feeling sad, read this list.

WEEK EIGHT

Appreciate the Scenery

Sometimes I am in such a hurry, I forget to look at the scenery, let alone appreciate it. Take the time necessary to appreciate the scenery, and you will enjoy your trip more. Take the time to appreciate others and you will enjoy your life more. That is what this week is all about.

My husband Paul and I used to teach a seminar for people considering remarriage, *Rethinking Marriage When Thinking Remarriage*. In preparation for that, we took a class for people preparing for marriage for the first time. We wanted to see if there was anything that could be adapted to our seminar.

One thing the instructor did was particularly helpful. We took a survey that really had an impact on both of us. It was a short version of The Meyers Briggs Type Indicator, called The Keirsey Temperament Sorter. What we learned that day changed our lives significantly. I learned that Paul was an introvert by nature. I was surprised because he always seemed so outgoing to me. It was no shock to Paul, however, that I was an extrovert. At that moment, we realized that we both had unrealistic expectations of the other.

I had preached *"acceptance"* for years, but that class helped me to take it to another level. I could not only accept Paul's personality traits but I could also learn to appreciate them for what they are-a wonderful complement to mine. Have you ever seen a color wheel? All the colors of the rainbow are on the wheel. The ones that are next to each other are very similar. The ones directly across the wheel, the opposites, are called complementary. That is how I began to look at Paul. He tends to be very practical. I am spontaneous. I need him to keep me from going off in too many directions. He needs me to keep him from stagnating. He told me the other day that he would be a hermit if it weren't for me.

What is your style?

Below you will find a survey I have developed. It is based closely on the behavioral styles first introduced by Hippocrates almost twenty-five centuries ago: Choleric, Phlegmatic, Melancholic and Sanguine. Please take a moment to complete the survey now. Put a check next to the phrases that describe you. When you're finished, follow the instructions at the end of the survey.

S	C
❑I am practical.	❑I do whatever looks like the most fun at the time.
❑I make decisions based on fact and logic.	❑I have lots of friends but I don't always keep in touch.
❑I have friends that I meet with regularly.	❑I am better at talking than listening.
❑I have a plan for every project	❑I make a party out of every project.
❑Emotions are a waste of time.	❑I seldom worry about anything.
❑I am very predicable.	❑I am always good for a laugh.
❑There is a right and wrong way of doing everything.	❑Doing things the same way gets boring.
❑I am always on time.	❑I am curious.
❑I expect people to make an appointment to see me.	❑I am often late; in fact, I often miss an appointment altogether.
❑I am logical.	❑I like to do things on the spur of the moment.
❑I don't waste time talking about it when things just need to get done.	❑I am fun.
❑ "The facts, ma'am, just the facts"	❑"The more the merrier!"

T	M
❐I make decisions quickly and easily ❐I have a definite set of close friends that share my approach to life. ❐I have high expectations of others. ❐I never let my emotions get in the way. ❐People always know what I think by the way that I act. ❐I do not tolerate tardiness in others and I lead by example. ❐I am usually right but not always popular. ❐I am aggressive. ❐I often have too much "on my plate". ❐I am determined. ❐I am good at being in charge. ❐"What have you done for me lately?"	❐I consider the feelings of others when making decisions. ❐I have a few close friends that I have known all my life. ❐ You can always count on me to help get things done. ❐I wear my emotions on my sleeve. ❐Most people know what I am feeling by the expression on my face. ❐I am compassionate. ❐Things don't always get done because I am so busy assisting others. ❐ I am sentimental. ❐ I can always find time for a friend. ❐ I think it is rude to be late. ❐ I am a very good listener. ❐"May I help you?"

Count the number of checks you have in each box and place your scores in the corresponding box below.

S	C	T	M
Total _____	Total _____	Total _____	Total _____

You may notice that you have a much higher number of checks in one or two boxes. Most people find that they are dominant in one or two areas. The labels at the top of each box have some significance.

I found the behavioral styles that Hippocrates developed 2500 years ago difficult to remember, so I decided to give each one a different name. Since I live in the Detroit Area and many of my clients are in the automotive industry, I decided to use different types of vehicles that correspond to the behavioral styles. I chose them based on the type of vehicle I thought each style might choose. You may not agree with the ones I chose; but if you read the explanation of each style, it will begin to make sense. When I tested the survey on more that 100 people, I found that about 75% who fit into each category were actually driving the corresponding vehicle. When asked if they had EVER driven the corresponding vehicle, another 10% said *"yes"*. Finally, when asked if they WISHED they owned the corresponding vehicle, another 5% admitted that they did. That means that as many as 90% of the people taking the survey fit into the respective categories. Here are the vehicles that correspond to the four types.

-   *S stands for Sedan.*
-   *C stands for Convertible.*
-   *T stands for Truck.*
-   *M stands for Mini-Van.*

Don't get hung up on the labels. The purpose of the survey is to help you understand yourself. This, in turn, might help you move from just acceptance to appreciation of others.

Sedan

Typically people who might drive a <u>*Sedan*</u> (Phlegmatic) have a strong need to do things right and by the book. In fact, they're the kind of people who actually read instruction manuals including the one in the car! The clock is always right, even the day after we change for daylight savings time. They like maps, charts and organization. Their four-door Sedan has a pocket for everything, and you can actually find things in their glove box. They are great at providing quality control for a home or office. They have deep feelings for those they love but sometimes have a hard time communicating that love. There are about the same percent of men and women in this category.

Convertibles

Most *Convertible* drivers (Sanguine) are excitable, fun seeking, cheer-leader types who love to talk. They are great at motivating others and need to be in an environment where they get to talk and have a vote on major decisions. They usually know people, who know people, who know people. The problem is that they hardly ever know anyone's name. They probably drive the convertible with the top down whenever possible. When it is cold out they just turn the heater up to full blast. They like to see and be seen. What better way to accomplish this than in a convertible? There is about a 50-50 mix of men and women in this category.

Trucks

The people who might own *Trucks* (Choleric) are take-charge lead-ers. They are usually the bosses at work, or at least they think they are. They are decisive, bottom line people who are not watchers or listeners. They love to solve problems. Trucks are vehicles that can be used for anything, anywhere, anytime…especially the 4X4 variety. They have deep feelings but are sometimes hard to get close to. If you have ever been behind one of these road hogs, it is next to impossible to pass them. They like being up front and higher than anyone else. About 75% of the people who fall into this category are men.

Mini-Vans

Those who would prefer to drive a *Mini-Van* (Melancholic) are absolutely reliable. They can absorb the most emotional pain in a rela-tionship and still stay committed. They are great listeners, empathizers, and encouragers. They are always looking out for others. That is possi-bly why they own a Mini-Van. That way they can give everyone a ride. They can, however, be such people-pleasers that they can have great dif-ficulty standing their ground when necessary. I am sure they were very excited when the automakers came up with separate heating and air conditioning controls for the driver and the passenger. That way everyone will be happy with the temperature. About 75% of the people who fit into this category are women.

You will have some characteristics in more than one category. In spite of the fact that you may be dominant in one area, you will probably still have some characteristics in the other areas as well. It is not about labeling or stereotyping. It is about understanding and moving from acceptance of other people's traits (just putting up with them) and appreciating them (or celebrating them.) The question begs to be asked, *"When the person I am dealing with is different, what value can I find in what they 'bring to the party'?"*

You might also notice that your dominant personality shifts in different environments. For instance, at work I want to be in charge (Truck). On vacation I always want to be a free spirit (Convertible). When we visit the kids I want to take care of everything (Mini-Van). I never want to pay attention to detail. That is why I appreciate people who do (Sedan).

What are the strengths and weaknesses of each style?

Each style has strengths. For almost every strength, there is a corresponding weakness. I have chosen one for each trait to illustrate this:

♦ Sedan Owners = Economical Vs Stingy
♦ Convertible Owners = Appealing Vs Egotistical
♦ Truck Owners = Leaders Vs Bossy
♦ Mini-Van Owners = Consistent Vs Resistant.

I have been called *"bossy"* and even *"overbearing by some"*, while others consider me a leader. When I was still single, I went out with a guy that I met at *Single Pointe*. He was tall, good-looking and by most women's standards, a good catch. We had a nice time on our date, and when he took me home, I asked him if he wanted to go for a walk. It was one of those beautiful summer evenings in Michigan. He agreed, so we started down the driveway, but when we arrived at the street, Dan started to the right. I stopped him and said, *"No, let's go this way,"* and pulled him to the left. He asked me if I always had to have my way and refused to go left. Here were two aggressive people ready for battle. I saw nothing wrong with my behavior, and I am sure he saw nothing wrong with his. Neither one of us stopped to find out the reasoning behind the other's choice. Mine was because the lake was to the left and it was a nicer walk. To this day I don't know his reason for wanting to go right. By the way, we never did go for a walk and we never went out again.

> *"For every strength there is a corresponding weakness."*

This incident was not particularly significant, but gives you a clear idea of the stubborn bent in Truck owners. A positive trait, *"Take Charge,"* can become a negative trait, *"Stubborn."* There have been many times that I have hurt someone I love with my natural tendencies. Perhaps you have taken one of your strengths to the extreme and turned it into a liability.

What can you do to understand others?

Understanding these traits can help us understand who we are and why our friends and loved ones behave as they do. Instead of thinking my way is best, I can understand that it's just *"my way"*. Others can have their way as well.

We actually need people who are different from ourselves. Stop for a moment and think of a person who is very different from you. Review the different traits with this in mind. One way to do this is to take the survey the way you think he/she would take it. While you may not be able to do this totally objectively, do your best. It may give you some insight. Perhaps the very thing that annoys you about this person is the thing that is most important to him/her. It might also be something you need in your life.

In my case, the traits that I found most repugnant in Paul were the things that I lacked. He really drives a four-door Sedan, and it is a compact one as well. It is not only practical but also economical. He pays attention to detail. His car has over 100 thousand miles on it and it looks like new. He never misses a bill payment of any kind. His closet is so organized that he could probably find his clothes in the dark. He is like my mother when it comes to money. He probably knows where his first dollar was spent.

As a contrast, I am naturally disorganized and, left to my own devices, would rather have a root canal than pay bills. I used to subscribe to the philosophy, *"If you want it, charge it."* Thanks to Paul, our only debt is our house and our credit is so good that we could borrow three times what we currently owe. My closet is now organized and although I couldn't find things in the dark, I do know where everything is.

By now, you have begun to see that there is a great difference between putting up with others and celebrating who they are. Celebrating who someone else is has given me so much more pleasure than trying to change someone. I used to seek approval. Now I give it. I know that I have developed some traits because of Paul. He has certainly helped me become a more well rounded person. I think, if you asked Paul, he would tell you that I have helped him to *"loosen up."* He has begun to enjoy some spontaneity in his life. He has also learned to splurge occasionally. We have really learned to appreciate each other.

Now that you understand yourself and others better, you can move from acceptance to appreciation.

How can you use this to get along with difficult people?

At one time or another, most of us could be called a difficult person. If I feel threatened or embarrassed, I find myself creating conflict, because I don't like to be questioned or put on the spot. No one really likes conflict. It doesn't matter if you're dealing with a marriage or a friendship, a relative or a co-worker, getting along is always better.

Here are five common reasons why people are difficult to get along with.

♦   Some people only feel good if they can look better than someone else.
♦   There is sometimes a strong need to be right all the time.
♦   Our society has cultivated the idea that we are not responsible for our feelings so other people can "make us mad."
♦   Some individuals expect others to meet *all* their needs.
♦   Busy lives push patience to the edge.

You may notice any or all of these in your own life and you certainly may observe them in others. But they don't give us an excuse to be difficult. Steven Covey, in *Seven Habits of Highly Effective People,* lists seven habits that could really help the human race get along better.

"Seek first to understand, then ask to be understood." Imagine what the world would be like if we all did that. He tells a marvelous story in chapter one:

> I remember a mini-paradigm shift I experienced one Sunday morning on a subway in New York. People were sitting quietly, some reading newspapers, some lost in thought, some resting with their eyes closed. It was a calm, peaceful scene.
>
> Then suddenly, a man and his children entered the subway car. The children were so loud and rambunctious that instantly the whole climate changed.
>
> The man sat down next to me and closed his eyes, apparently oblivious to the situation. The children were yelling back and forth, throwing things, even grabbing people's papers. It was very disturbing and yet the man sitting next to me did nothing. It was difficult not to feel irritated. I could not believe that he

could be so insensitive as to let his children run wild like that and do nothing about it, taking no responsibility at all. It was easy to see that everyone else on the subway felt irritated, too. So finally, with what I felt was unusual patience and restraint, I turned to him and said, "Sir, your children are really disturbing a lot of people. I wonder if you couldn't control them a little more?"

The man lifted his gaze as if to come to a consciousness of the situation for the first time and said softly, "Oh, you're right. I guess I should do something about it. We just came from the hospital where their mother died about an hour ago. I don't know what to think and I guess they don't know how to handle it either."

Can you imagine what I felt at that moment? My paradigm shifted. Suddenly I *saw* things differently, and because I saw things differently, I thought differently, I felt differently, I behaved differently. My irritation vanished. I didn't have to worry about controlling my attitude or my behavior; my heart was filled with the man's pain. Feelings of sympathy and compassion flowed freely. "Your wife just died? Oh, I'm so sorry. Can you tell me about it? What can I do to help?" Everything changed in an instant.

It is so easy to choose a negative reaction to a situation because of what it looks like on the surface. The last difficult person you encountered may not have a good excuse like this young man, but you still have a choice about how you will respond. Are you willing to let the situation control you?

> *"Seek first to understand; then ask to be understood." Stephen Covey*

Make amends. You meet difficult people wherever you go. Many of the difficult people we meet are just being themselves. And any positive trait pushed to its limit becomes a liability. With busy lives, it's, it's easier to become irritable and hard to get along with than it is to be kind. Compassion will serve you better in the end.

Here are some things you can do to make situations more tolerable and maybe even turn them around.

1. Consider what the difficult person (DP) is going through. Are there stresses that exacerbate the conflict? Is he/she under pressure at home/work?

2. Consider your own mood or mindset. Are you under stress or pressure? Are you over-reacting?

3. Consider the basic personality of the DP. Is he in a position that is incompatible with his personality? Is he an extrovert with a research job? Is he an introvert with a sales job?

4. Make an offer to be part of the solution. One way to do this is to approach the DP and express your desire to work things out.

5. Make sure she knows that you believe that *"what's right is more important than who's right."*

You will see immediately that these steps are *"seeking to understand"* others. Now you can begin to choose an approach for dealing with the DP.

Use feel, felt, found. There is a great technique used in sales called *"feel, felt, found."* Here is how it works. You start by saying, *"I understand how you feel, others have felt that way, too. And this is what they found."* This may be a little too scripted for you, but it really works. You begin by telling the DP how you understand how he/she feels. Next, you tell him/her that others have felt the same way and you end by recounting a story of how others have seen it differently.

I used *"feel, felt, found"* recently during a workshop when a man responded to my comments on reflective listening by saying, *"Parroting back what my wife said is stupid."*

"I can understand how you <u>feel</u>," I responded. *"Lots of people <u>feel</u> that way at first because it seems so awkward. In fact, my husband <u>felt</u> the same way you do. And what he <u>found</u> was that coming up with some phrases of his own works better for him. He says 'It sounds like you...or 'That must really feel....'"* Then I asked the group to share how it felt to be the recipient of the reflective listening. Several people raised their hands and said that they felt *"validated,"* *"affirmed,"* and *"knew their partner was listening."* I am not sure if this man ever agreed with me about reflective listening. That was not my goal. I wanted him to know that I understood his perspective.

Find a place where we agree. Here is a story that illustrates this view. There was a little boy named Jimmy who was constantly being picked on by a bully at school. Every day he would come home in tears. His mother offered a suggestion and the next day Jimmy put it to the test. On the way home, sure enough, the bully stopped Jimmy in his tracks. With all the courage he could muster, Jimmy drew a line in the dirt just like his mother had told him and said boldly, *"I dare you to step over that line."* The bully looked at him in amazement and not surprisingly stepped over the line. Quickly, Jimmy put his arm around the bully's shoulder and said, *"Now, we are both on the same side."*

Well this might not work with a schoolyard bully but it will work with most people. See if you can find something to agree upon...something where you can be on the same side.

Establish a common ground. In *Getting to Yes: Negotiating Agreement Without Giving In,* Roger Fisher et al demonstrate the power of establishing common ground even if you don't agree with someone. In this way you eliminate the need to argue and open the door for improved cooperation. People who are ready for an argument are totally disarmed when you tell them *"yes."* I sometimes imagine it this way: DPs are all set up to push against a wall of disagreement that others have set up. When you don't put up that wall, they keep moving, right toward you.

I taught my son this technique when he was in elementary school. He was getting into arguments at school with some of his classmates. I don't know if he ever used the technique at school, but he sure used it on me. One day I sent him to clean his room, and an hour later I found him on the bedroom floor, playing with his Legos. Boy, was I mad. I started in on him like the demanding person I am. He looked up at me with those big brown eyes and said, *"You're right, Mom. I should have been cleaning my room instead of playing with my Legos. If I were you, I would be mad, too. I am sorry. I will clean it up now."* I just had to laugh out loud. The steam was gone from my anger and I even helped him finish cleaning his room.

Laugh now, not later. Now let's look at the second point. When you find yourself in conflict with a DP, what's your mood at the time? Are you tired…stressed…upset about something else over which you have no control? All of these things can contribute to our response. Perhaps at another time or another place the same event would not affect you negatively. You might even laugh about it.

My friend Kathy once told me about her mother's great comeback whenever anyone said, *"You know, we will probably laugh about this someday."* Her mother would ask, *"Why wait?"* She told me this when I was going through some difficult times. One Christmas, Kathy's mother gave everyone a sweatshirt that said, *"If you're gonna laugh about it later, why wait?"* The waitress I mentioned earlier was in no way the worst waitress I had ever had. She became a difficult person in my mind because *I* was having a bad day. So taking a few deep breaths, taking a walk, or maybe even laughing may take the sting out of your experience with DP's.

Consider the personality of the Difficult Person. Let's look at how each type handles challenges. The Truck owner has a need to be right. He sees himself as the leader and when that is challenged he is ready for a fight, especially if cornered. You've met the type: *"My way or the highway."*

Convertible owners will tend to make a joke out of everything. That can be maddening when you are trying to have a serious discussion. *"Did I tell you about the time when...?"* It is sometime difficult to get these people to the point of resolution.

The people who own Mini Vans will try to make everyone happy. That might seem great, but it can keep things from being resolved. The conflict may emerge later, even more intense, if you don't take care of it now. *"Now, don't cry, Dear. Let's not talk about it right now. Everything will be all right."*

The Sedan owner will be the most logical in a conflict. All conflicts cannot be solved with logic, however. He/she can come across as cold and uncaring. *"Give me the facts, ma'am, just the facts."*

Of course, *your* personality plays a role in the conflict as well. If you read one of the quotes above and thought, *"Well, what's so bad about that?"* you are probably that particular type. Of course, nobody's just one temperament. I am an Truck owner at work, a Convertible owner with friends, and I drive a Mini Van for my children and grandson.

When I am exhibiting one style, the other temperaments can drive me crazy. For instance, at work I don't have much patience with Convertible Owners. It is time to get some work done, not play games. Looking at the situation from the DP's perspective can make a difference.

The more important the relationship, the more effort you may be willing to put into it. No matter how unimportant the relationship, if you are willing to put forth some effort...to be the one to take the first step, you will reap the rewards. In our *"looking out for number One"* society, this is not very popular but it is rewarding.

What is your personality? You may have a very high score in two areas. You may be fairly balanced. Whatever your style, are there people in your life you find difficult to get along with? It may be because he is exhibiting a trait that you find irritating simply because you are dominant in a different style.

Use reflective listening. Here are two things to choose from the next time you find yourself in conflict. Reflect back to the person what they just said from your perspective. Use *"feel, felt, found."* Consider their challenges, your mood and both of your personalities. Practice this soon and write down what happened. I think you will be surprised at the results.

Another way to handle this is to reflect back to the person what just happened in a neutral, story fashion. When my friend's teenage daughter was being particularly demanding one day, she said, *"Here's what I see. One day a 14-year-old demanded that her mother drop everything she was doing and take her to Wal-Mart, buy her a list of specific things, run her to her friend's house, wait while she dropped a few things off, and then take her home."* Mother and daughter both started laughing, and they figured out an alternative plan. Sometimes, with your help using reflective listening, people can step back and look at the situation from a new perspective.

When people are being difficult, they are often simply being themselves. That doesn't mean his/her behavior is a good thing. It just means that before I get irritated with someone, I want to stop and think. Is he doing this *"to"* me, or am I just being intolerant? Most of the time it is the latter. I only have control over what I choose, not what the other person chooses. The secret to getting along with difficult people is choosing to understand and responding with kindness and not anger.

Suggestions for Action this week:

1.   Make a list of the significant people in your life…those that have the most influence.
2.   Next to each name list the things you appreciate about them and why.
3.   Make a *"date"* with each person and tell him or her what you wrote.

4. Make a journal entry about each experience.
5. Make a list of some difficult people in your life.
6. Write down why you consider them difficult.
7. Examine each entry by asking yourself these questions:
8. Is there something going on in this person's life that may be affecting them in a negative way?
9. What is the main personality style of this person? And how does it compare to mine?
10. Write down some alternatives to getting irritated with this person.
11. Begin to practice some of the alternatives.

Respect the Rules of the Road

If you don't respect the rules of the road, you might end up having an accident. If you don't respect others, you might end up without much respect for yourself. There is no more important human need than respect. This week, you will learn some simple ways to show more respect for others and therefore get more respect from others.

Some of my coaching clients are general managers of luxury car dealerships. One of their major concerns is customer satisfaction. We have often discussed how to increase it. There is something that costs little or no money and would increase customer satisfaction overnight: show respect to all of your customers and your employees. That is what most people want, no matter what their status...*respect*. A little respect can make just about everyone feel better.

I have collected good and bad customer service stories over the years. The common thread in every single one is a desire for respect. This is not limited to employees not respecting customers. I have seen, however, that some customers do not show respect for the employee. Whose job is it to start giving respect? Both. I have threatened to write a book on how to *get* great customer service instead of how to deliver it. I have never written it because I don't think any customer would read it. But if

I had, the whole book would have been about showing respect. Maybe you don't think a rude waitress deserves respect. Have you ever considered what happens to *you* when you are disrespectful?

What does being disrespectful do for you?

Notice the next time you get angry with someone and respond in a rude manner. If you took your blood pressure, it would be higher than normal. Your heart usually beats faster and harder. That's good for you when you are exercising, but not when it comes from anger or rage.

My son and I were at a restaurant once when he was about ten years old. I had had a bad day and things were not going well. I ended up scolding the waitress for her lack of service. After we had paid the bill and I was headed out to the car, something made me stop. I was disappointed in how I had behaved. I needed to go back and apologize to the waitress. What was I teaching my son with that behavior? It took all the courage I could muster to go back and apologize. I will never know if it helped her, but it certainly helped me.

How can you show respect?

Now, I make it a practice when I am getting bad service to tell the person not to worry. I am going to be the easiest person they have ever waited on. It usually gets me better service and even if it doesn't, I feel better because I am not angry. There are many other ways to show respect. Here are some of mine.

> *"There is no more important human need than respect."*

Be on time. I have an old friend that is habitually late. We always tell him 7:00 when we really mean 7:30. Only now he's figured us out, so he is still late. In today's fast-paced world, everyone is busy. My time is valuable and so is yours. When I'm late, I'm not showing respect. Of course, there are extenuating circumstances from time to time. After all, we are all human. If you are often late, you show disrespect. Consider this a target for change.

One way to do this is by planning ahead. If you get distracted easily, then set a timer or alarm clock to remind you it is time to leave. You can also get some help from a friend or family member. A gentle reminder might just do the trick. Once you get into the habit of being on time, you will be amazed how much more peaceful your life will become.

Do what you said you would do. This can encompass being on time, but there are other areas to consider as well. Someone I love dearly had a father that always said he was going to do great things with and for his family. For instance, his father was always going to take all the family to Disneyland. He never did. He was always going to take his sons hunting. He never did. Imagine what it was like growing up with this.

If you have a hard time living up to your commitments, then reexamine your commitments. In your interest to make people happy, maybe you are over-committing. I used to teach a class for single adults, and one of the major complaints I got from women was the fact that men always promised to call and never did. It could have been about over committing. The respectful thing is to follow through, even when it is painful. By this I mean, if you promise to do something, have enough respect to call if you can't live up to your commitment.

"Let your 'yes' be 'yes' and your 'no' be 'no'!"

Sometimes people commit to things because they have a hard time saying "no". They don't want to hurt someone's feelings. If you know that you will not be able to what you are about to commit to, then don't commit.

Be interested in others. When having a conversation with someone, ask questions about what is going on in his or her life. If there is anything that makes people feel important, it is talking about themselves. This is probably the best way to give validation, because everyone has a story to tell. Think about the last time you had a long conversation with someone and all he talked about was himself. Did you wonder if he was ever going to ask what was going on in your life? Show people that you respect them by talking about what is interesting to them. Be interested. Your friends will love it and know that you care.

Listen well. When someone is telling you his or her story, just stop talking and listen with all your heart. You will be astonished at how people really need to talk—and you may just be the angel that will hear them for the first time. A good way to show them that you are listening is by using the following technique. Repeat back to your friend what they just told you. For example, someone tells you about a hectic day he or she just had. You come back with something like this; *"It sounds like you have had a really rough day."*

> *"No agreeing, disagreeing, judging or fixing!"*

It might sound too simple but it works. I teach this technique in some of my seminars. After they have had a chance to use it, I ask them how it felt to be on the receiving end of this type of listening. Without exception, I have people say things like, *"I felt like he really understood how I felt."* Or, *"It felt like she really cared about me."* One rule I give them is no agreeing, disagreeing, judging or fixing. Not only does the speaker feel more understood and cared for, but the listener becomes a better listener. I can't worry about what I am going to say next if I know I have to repeat what the speaker is saying.

Admit your mistakes. It is amazing how hard it is to admit that I was wrong and how great I feel after I do. The person I hurt feels better, too. What more can you ask for? Forgiveness might not come right away, but you can know that you have done the right thing by admitting your mistake and asking for forgiveness.

There are some very important things to consider. When admitting your mistake, your tone of voice really matters. If you sound like you are angry about your admission, it takes the value away. The wording is also important. Saying, "*If I hurt you, then I am sorry.*" is not admitting that you made a mistake. It puts the onus on the other person. It is probably already obvious that you hurt him or her. Saying something like, "*I can tell that you are hurting. I am so sorry that I caused that hurt,*" is much more healing.

Be willing to change. Admitting your mistake is worthless if you are not willing to stop making the same one over and over again. Saying you're sorry is not enough. You must be willing to make an effort to stop doing what is hurtful to the other person. It is not always easy to make that change but that is what this book is all about. You can make changing this type of behavior the focus for one of your thirteen weeks.

Stop sharing derogatory information about others. Believe it or not, there are at least three people who loose when you spend time complaining about someone. You suffer because you are spending your time and energy doing something that does not increase your value in any way. The person/s listening to you will either join in or look down on you. Either choice is not helpful to anyone. Finally, the person you are talking about will suffer because you are spreading unfavorable information. Even if the information is true, telling someone else will never help them see the error of their ways. I suggest going to the person and discussing how you feel with him/her directly. There is no guarantee that he or she will change, but at least you will know that you did the right thing.

You will be amazed how much better you feel about yourself when you make an effort to show respect toward others.

Suggestions for Action this week:

1. Observe people and notice what they do to show respect/disrespect.
2. Write about what you see in your journal.
3. Notice when people do and do not show you respect.
4. Write about how this feels in your journal.

5.   Imagine how others feel when some one treats him/her with respect/disrespect.
6.   Find an opportunity to show respect to someone this week.
7.   Write in your journal about how you feel after you do this.

WEEK TEN

Anticipate Rush Hour

This chapter was hard for me to write because I am not naturally an organized person. Being organized enough to anticipate rush hour was only a dream just a few years ago. I had to work at it every day. When I didn't, I got behind and lost time. In *Getting Things Done*, Edwin C. Bliss said that every ten minutes you spend planning saves you an hour. Because I am a *"doing"* person by nature, it is hard for me to take the time to plan. However, I find I have much more time when I plan and you can too, even if you resist it like I do.

> *"Every ten minutes you spend planning can save you an hour!"*

What tools do you need?

There are many tools to help make planning easier. The most widely used is the *"To Do List"*. You may use a printed form or the back of an old envelope. Taking it one step further, you may have a calendar or planner. Perhaps the best known is the Franklin Planner. There are others on the market: Day Timer, Day Runner, and Day-at-a-Glance, just to name a few.

If you want to use a planner, I recommend you get an inexpensive one at first to find out what works for you. As I mentioned earlier, I used to teach the corporate version of the Franklin Covey System. I like their system and it works for me, but at first I resisted even the idea of trying it. I didn't want to become rigid. I quickly learned, though, that I was able to be more spontaneous when I was organized. When I am more organized, I don't have to spend time worrying about what I have forgotten. That way, I actually am free to enjoy my spare time instead of wondering if I have forgotten something.

Now, I use a Palm Pilot. It is a small, Personal Digital Assistant (PDA). There are other PDAs on the market but this was one of the first. I still use the Franklin Covey System, but not on paper. There is software that allows me to plan my day on my desktop and then download it (or Hotsync it) to the Palm Pilot. Whatever you use, don't buy anything expensive until you find what really works for you. All PDAs are small and portable, but can turn into very expensive address books if you don't use them properly.

What can you do to prioritize?

Making a "To Do List" while planning your day is only the first step in getting organized. The next step is prioritizing. If you are busy all day but not accomplishing much, perhaps you are spending time on things that are not really important. The key to working smarter is deciding what you want to accomplish and doing the things that will make it happen.

Steven Covey uses a system that I like, a box with four quadrants. The top left-hand box is labeled Urgent /Important. All crises and deadline driven projects fall in this quadrant. For instance, if you wait too long to get an oil change for your vehicle, it will be both urgent and important. The top right hand box is labeled Not Urgent/Important. If you get an oil change when it is scheduled, it is important but not yet urgent. The bottom left-hand quadrant is Not Important/Urgent. This would include things that are unavoidable and prevent you from doing something important. Interruptions fall into this category. Finally, the bottom right hand quadrant is Not Important/Not Urgent. This can be for trivial activities like opening junk mail.

Determine the time wasters. I ask my coaching clients to make a list of everything they do for one week in fifteen-minute increments. Don't panic! I know it sounds overwhelming, but it is only for a week. Once you finish, you will be amazed at how much you do that you consider a waste of time. The best place to find time is in the Not Important/Not Urgent category. Things that fall into that quadrant could be eliminated or delegated.

Do things before they become urgent. The things that are Important and Urgent must be done, but if you can prevent important things from becoming urgent, you will have a lot less stress. Let's look at the oil change example I used in the last paragraph. Most cars need an oil change every three thousand miles. When you have driven your car 2,800 miles since your last oil change, it is neither important nor urgent to get an oil change. Even at 3,200 miles it is not urgent but it is probably getting to be important. If you wait until 5,000, it is now getting to be urgent *and* important.

Every time you get into your car, you will probably think, *"I need an oil change, but I don't have time!"* It causes stress. If you had had the oil changed somewhere between 2,800 and 3,200 miles it would not have been so urgent and would not have been as stressful. *"But I didn't have time then, either,"* you say. However, you will have to take the time now or risk ruining your engine. Once you get more organized, you can start to do the things that are important and not urgent. Do first things first! You may even enjoy not having to scramble every time something important is due.

"Do first things first!"

Write everything in your planner. Have you ever found a piece of paper with a phone number on it but no name and wonder whose it was? You know you wrote it down for a reason, but you can't remember why. It is very frustrating. When I used a paper planner, I had one with two pages for every day. I used my planner to write everything. I even wrote directions on the date that I would need them. If you gave me directions to your office and I was going to meet you at your office on Saturday, I would turn to Saturday and write the directions there. I wouldn't have to look all over for the directions on Saturday because they were right there where I needed them.

Now, I go to the internet and download a map right into my PDA. Having everything in one place has saved me so much time. With the PDA, it is all backed up on my computer. That way I don't even have to worry about losing my planner.

How can you keep track of everything?

If you have a spouse or children, I'm sure the following has happened to you. One day your boss asks you to do something after work on a particular day next week. You agree to do it and enter it on your calendar at work. You get home and realize that your son's little league championship game is scheduled for that very same day. Your boss would have understood if you mentioned it at the outset, but now you have to go back and change everything or disappoint your son. Neither choice is very appealing.

Use one calendar. If you had put everything on a planner that you kept with you all the time, then you could have checked before you agreed to stay late on any day. This technique will make your life much simpler. E. M. Gray, author of the *Common Denominator of Success*, said, *"The successful person has the habit of doing the things failures/unsuccessful people don't like to do/don't do. Successful people don't like them either but they put that dislike away and do it anyway."*

Maybe you are ready to do something you don't necessarily like but know will bring you great satisfaction once you have mastered it.

Plan your day before it starts. Planning your day, every day, will help keep you on track. I do this is the morning. Some of my clients with small children plan at night after they are all in bed asleep. No matter when you choose to plan, it is important to do it before you start your day. It is also important to make sure you put things on your list that apply to every area in your life that you are working on. Referring back to the Balance Wheel on page 20, you can take a look at the areas that are important to you. Set some goals in that area. Include something on your daily task list every day that will get you closer to the desired end. *"A journey of a thousand miles begins with one step."* You can take a single step today.

Planning is the key to getting things done. Find a tool that works for you and use it every day. Keep everything in one place and only use one calendar. Make sure you include something that will get you closer to the goals you have set for yourself. A journey of a thousand miles begins with one step. Start today by using your time wisely.

Suggestions for Action this week:

1. Go to your local office supply store and check out the planners.
2. Choose an inexpensive one to use for a while.
3. Make a plan for the day in your planner every day.
4. Mark the items that are most important.
5. Do the important ones first every day.
6. The ones that don't get done, move to the next day, delegate them or eliminate them.
7. Have a friend/coach hold you accountable.
8. Write in your journal about how using some of these principles helps you get things done.

Complete Routine Maintenance

While routine maintenance is usually a priority with your car, you may neglect taking care of yourself. You may have heard of someone who is considered a success in business but never has any time for herself and is in very poor health. That is not what I consider success. You can't be much good for anyone else if you don't take care of yourself first. This is about good self-care.

What are the right supplements for you?

There is a lot of debate about eating right and taking the right supplements. One school of thought is that if you eat right you will not need to take supplements. Consider this: I heard from a nutritionist that the U.S. Agricultural Department has determined that the fruit and vegetables that we eat today have about 40% of the nutritional value that they had just 20 years ago. If this is true, then we would have to eat 60% more to get the same vitamins and minerals.

> *"Some people take better care of their cars that they do themselves."*

I believe in taking supplements instead. Personally, I use vitamins that are designed just for me. About once a year, I send a urine sample to a lab where it is analyzed to determine the right mix of vitamins, minerals, and amino acids for me. Then once a month I get a box in the mail with thirty little packets of capsules. I call them my designer vitamins. Recently, this has become much more affordable. When I started doing this fifteen years ago, the lab test cost over $100. I have heard of people paying over $200 today. One company, Ideal Health, offers the Priva-Test for $79. If you are interested, check with your chiropractor, doctor or fitness instructor. They may be able to help you find out where you can have this type of test done in your area. The vitamins cost about $56 a month. This is a lot less than I would pay if I went to the health food store and bought all the things that are included in the capsules designed for me. And then I wouldn't even know whether I was getting the right things or the right amounts.

What is the right weight for you?

Have you ever heard of someone who lost 40 pounds eating eggs and grapefruit three times a day and someone else who gained 40 pounds on the same diet? Well, there is a reason. We are all a little different. In his book, *The Weight is Over*; Dr. Jack Tips explains the importance of understanding our individual metabolism. *"The big question is: 'What are the right ratios (of the three macro-nutrients: protein, fat, and carbohydrate) for you? How do you find the magic balance that will unlock your fat burning mechanism when your metabolism is unique?'"*

He goes on to explain: *"Our individual biochemistry dictates the proper ration of these macro-nutrients for a balanced hormonal response that can stop storing fat and start burning it."* He recommends a simple lab test called the FitTest to pinpoint your particular metabolism. Another source for discovering your unique metabolic needs is by taking a survey that uses standards established by comparing several laboratory tests. Mannatech has a survey for this purpose. It can be taken online by visiting their website.

Once you find out what proportion of proteins, carbohydrates and fat that is best for you, you will be pleasantly surprised. If you begin to eat right for your unique metabolic make up, you will feel better, and you will have more energy. You may even improve your outlook on life. Many people even find that their weight begins to stabilize because they are eating better. It is worth the effort. Exercise might even become appealing.

What exercise is right for you?

Speaking of exercise, this might not seem like a great way to be good to yourself, but it is. Imagine owning a high performance racecar and never driving it over 35 MPH. What a waste! Muscles were designed to be used; yet today most people in America and perhaps around the world live very sedentary lives. When was the last time you broke a sweat? If you don't remember, then you had better look at your lifestyle.

Our grandparents probably did not have to make an effort to fit physical exertion into their daily lives. They worked hard physically every day, and it showed in their physical and mental health. Today, many of us are too busy to use our muscles to improve our health.

You may benefit from having a fitness coach. Maybe you just need a buddy, or to set up a schedule that includes regular exercise. Whatever you need to do, find a way to include some type of physical exertion in your weekly routine. It does not take much. In fact, simply adding as little as five minutes every other day, every week for the next thirteen weeks, will put you ahead of millions of Americans.

It can even be fun. If the thought of a "stairclimber" makes you shudder, then ride a bike…out in the fresh air. If time is a real challenge, then look for ways to increase your activity within your daily schedule. How about parking in the last parking space and walking further to the office? How about climbing the stairs instead of taking the elevator? Of course, it does take a little more time, but it,s a lot less time than going to the gym and sweating for an hour, showering, dressing and going back to work. Besides, to quote Dr. Tips again, *"Muscles burn fat and more muscle burns more fat."* And you don't have to look like Arnold

Swarzenegger to make this happen. A simple walk every day will do the trick. And you just might learn to love it.

What can you do to get enough sleep?

So now you are eating right, taking a good nutritional supplement and exercising regularly. What else can you do to take care of yourself?

First, make sure you get a good night's sleep; second, drink enough good clean water; and third, make sure you have clean air in your home! Eating right and exercising will help you sleep better—and so will a good mattress.

My husband Paul has been in the furniture business for over ten years, and he reports that people do not want to spend much on their mattress. Think about it. You spend one third of your life sleeping. In fact, you spend more time there than you do on almost any other piece of furniture. Why wouldn't you want to have the best possible place to sleep? Have you ever wakened with your arm asleep? Do you wake with a backache? Do you snore? All of these can prevent your getting proper rest. Conventional wisdom says that we need to sleep at least eight hours each night, but that is not universal. In fact, some of us need more. The point is that we need sound, restful sleep. Without it, our bodies do not have time to repair and refresh.

My husband and I have had great results with a pillow top mattress. To me, it is like sleeping on a cloud. This type of mattress is firm under the pillow top so there is great support. Sometimes I hate to leave home because I have to sleep on another mattress! I also have a mattress pad and a pillow from Nikken, Inc. They use magnetic therapy. I am not sure *how* it works—but it works. When I am traveling, if I forget to take my mattress pad and pillow with me, I really notice the difference.

> *"You can't be much good to anyone else if you
> don't take care of yourself first."*

How much and what kind of water should you drink?

Have you noticed how much bottled water there is on the store shelves today? Well, there is a reason. Water—without additives—is better for you than any other liquid. Not all bottled water is good, but it is better than carbonated beverages. There are several different schools of thought on how much and what type of water you should drink, but most experts agree that water is the best thing you can do for your body at the cellular level. Our body is made up of 90% water so it stands to reason that we need to have lots of water to make up for the loss we experience every day through elimination.

Typically, when you balance your proteins and carbohydrates, your body will demand more water. According to Krystal Gray, Certified Clinical Nutritionist, it is critical to drink enough each day to supply your cells with enough water to function properly. A good rule of thumb is to drink about one ounce of water for every pound you weigh. For instance, if you weigh 130 pounds, you need to drink about 130 ounces per day. Before you freak out about drinking that much water, realize that that is only about eight large glasses of water. If you start early, then you won't be up all night.

However, when you first start you will need to "use the facilities" more often. Be patient; your body will get used to it. If you are worried about water weight gain, stop. Drinking lots of water is one of the best ways to eliminate water retention.

The kind of water you drink is also very important. Some people believe in distilled water because it is free of additives and harmful chemicals. It is also free of minerals that are usually present in the clear spring water that you find in the mountains. Don't be fooled by the bottled water that is called spring water either. Read the label. Some bottled water is only tap water from a municipal water system.

In our home, we use a reverse osmosis system from Culligan on our tap water to make sure the impurities are taken out. There are other systems, like Nikken's PiMag and Alpine Industries' Living Water that use additional technology to enhance the water you drink. You can even buy inexpensive distillers if you are interested in distilled water. The point is mainly to drink more water—the cleaner and purer, the better.

What is important about the air you breathe?

Finally, make sure the air in your home is clean. There has been a lot of talk recently about indoor air. With improved insulation and well-sealed windows, homes are almost airtight. That may be good for the utility bill but not for your lungs. Any airborne bacteria just keep recirculating. You may have noticed that you get the flu without even coming in contact with an infected person. If you work in a building that has no windows that open, you may notice how everyone seems to keep passing around an illness.

The reason may be that the bacteria have attached themselves to the particles in the air. You don't notice these particles, but they are there.

The next time you see the sun shining through a window, look at the stream of light. The particles are small, and you inhale some of them every time you breathe. There are special filters for the fan on your furnace and air conditioner. These may help some but they can also trap contaminants after a while and actually introduce bacteria into your indoor air. There are also portable hepa-filters. They have the same problem and the filters are very expensive.

I prefer an air *purifier* not a *filter*. Alpine Industries and Sharper Image both have one that works well. There are no filters to replace, and that can save you a great deal of money. The only maintenance is cleaning a metal or glass plate once a month. Another way to get some fresh air is to sleep with a window open. Even when it is very cold outside, a small crack in the window will give you some much-needed clean air. There have actually been studies that show that the air in our home is worse than the air outside that everyone keeps worrying about. This seems to be much more important in the winter when people spend less time outside.

All of these things: eating right, taking supplements, exercising, getting a good night's sleep, drinking pure water, and breathing good clean air might seem to be a big adjustment. If so, take it one step at a time. Pick one area to focus on and start there. Once you have tackled that one, move on to the next. Making the choice based on your needs is probably the best way to start.

What about having some fun?

I have notice that many people really don't have much fun anymore. You always hear that technology has given us increased leisure time, but from my perspective, all technology has done is give us more opportunity to "be productive." Well, having fun is productive for our health. Now you might think it is fun to play video games or go to a movie. But what about an old fashioned picnic? How about a hike in the mountains? What about a bike ride in the park?

When was the last time you read a book...just for fun? My husband loves to fish. What do *you* love to do that is really fun? It doesn't have to cost a lot of money. Even if you can afford something lavish, what can you do to help *you* appreciate the simpler things in life? Paul and I go on weekend trips as often as possible. Most of the time we drive, just to be together and enjoy the scenery. That way, the journey there can be fun. We sometimes have our best conversations in the car. And I like to stay in Bed and Breakfasts. The food is usually very good, and the room is most often more affordable than a hotel. Having fun means feeling more relaxed when you're done. Take a break—long or short.

The Italians have *reposo*. Mexicans have the *siesta*. What do Americans have? A coffee break! Reposo and siestas last for hours. A coffee break lasts for fifteen minutes. And drinking coffee actually causes stress on your body and can make you gain weight by causing an insulin reaction. Plan more relaxation and fun in your life.

The bottom line is eat right, take a good nutritional supplement, exercise, drink water, get enough rest, breathe fresh clean air and have some fun. That is my prescription for taking care of yourself.

Suggestions for Action this week:

1. Keep track of what you eat for one week.
2. Research what is right for your metabolic profile.
3. Find and take a good nutritional supplement.
4. Add five minutes of exercise to your daily routine three days a week for the next thirteen weeks.
5. Drink more water and avoid coffee or carbonated beverages.
6. Keep a sleep log for 30 days.
7. Sleep with your window open.
8. Add something fun to your daily "to-do" list.

WEEK TWELVE

Safeguard Your Finances

When we take a trip, we always set aside some money to pay for it. I have always thought that was a good idea. However, until I met Paul, I never knew how to extend this to my life. We now have an approach that works well for us: Make as much as you can; save as much as you can; give as much as you can. You can adapt this to fit your lifestyle and safeguard your finances, not just for a trip, but for the rest of your life.

I believe that one of the reasons that my siblings and I don't have to worry about my mother financially is that she has been frugal all her life. As I mentioned before, she had a substantial savings account when my father died. Together they never made a fantastic living, but my mom always saved everything she could. As a result, she can afford to do a lot of things other people her age cannot do.

> *"Make as much as you can. Save as much as you can. Give as much as you can."*

My mother tried to teach me how to handle money. It wasn't until I was almost forty years old that I began to recognize the wisdom of her philosophy. After we were married, Paul suggested that we take a seminar about how to manage our personal finances. I don't think he needed the class but I did. Because of that class we adopted a three-pronged rule: *"Make as much as we can, save as much as we can, and give as much as we can.*" We have been married for fifteen years at the writing of this book and we are in better financial shape than we have ever been. I don't know if you would call us rich but we are very happy with our net worth in spite of the so-called economic downturn.

What can you do to make more money?

There are only two ways to do better financially: either make more or spend less. Paul and I both have variable incomes. He is a commissioned sales person. I am a self-employed speaker, coach and author. We both work very hard, but it is difficult to know exactly how much income we will have every month. That is the downside. The upside is the fact that if we want more money, we don't have to change jobs. We can just work harder or longer hours. Not everyone has that flexibility.

Get a promotion. One way to increase your income is to get a promotion. I work with a lot of executives who want to move up in the corporation. It involves more responsibility and substantially more money. Sometimes it requires additional education or training. Strategizing with someone who can help you decide the best route to take can be very helpful.

Change jobs. There seems to be a policy within some organizations that unless you change jobs you can't get a salary increase. In some cases, changing companies is the only way you can increase your income. Be aware of the consequences that might occur if you change jobs too often. You might be perceived as undependable.

Build seniority and/or get additional education. Some occupations have pay raises attached to seniority. For example, when I was a teacher, we received a pay raise every year for eleven years. Additional education also brought additional income. In some cases, getting an undergraduate or graduate degree is the only way to make more money. Be aware that higher education comes with a high cost. Make sure that if you invest in this strategy that it will give you a good return on your investment.

Get a second job. Another way to increase your income is by getting a second job. It is important to choose something that will not put you under too much pressure. I had a job delivering papers once. I had to get up at 2:30 A.M. but it was not taxing mentally. I didn't have to think, and I made some much-needed extra income. This one could easily be done while you still have another job, provided you can still get enough sleep. In that job, I was done by 7:00 A.M. That was plenty of time for me to make it to a second job. Be aware that such a choice may put a strain on your relationships. If you know it is temporary, say until you get some short-term debt paid off, it can be tolerable.

Own your own business. Owning your own business is also an option. It can be very expensive but also very profitable. I would recommend a small business coach if you were thinking of trying this solution. My friend Susan Linan opened a small wallpaper/window treatment store called *All for Walls*. She is the only one who works there so she doesn't have much overhead expense. Even though it is a small place it is still a lot of work. However, she loves it and is making a better living than she was when she worked for someone else. If you pick the right business it can work very well for you.

My hairdresser and her husband have a great business. He works for one of the automakers during the week and installs garage storage units on the weekends. His product is shown at home improvement shows by the manufacturer, and he gets the leads. However, doing this can put a strain on relationships. There is little time for anything else when you own your own business and work full time. If you have employees, it can be even more difficult. Before you jump into a business, make sure you know all the good and bad points. That way you can make an educated choice.

Own a business with your spouse. I know a coach who specializes in helping couples who work together learn how to do it well. Her name is Kari Hunter. She lives in the Chicago area and coaches all around the country via telephone. According to Kari, the number one mistake among entrepreneurial couples is that they take time to analyze, strate-gize, and plan for the success of their business but they DON'T do the same for their relationship. She says, "Fostering and nurturing a strong relationship will give life and positive energy to any joint business endeavor making it more likely to succeed."

Start a home-based business. There is huge growth in this industry. This is one way to own a business with a lot less expense.

There are lots of businesses that lend themselves to being based in your home. Writing and Editing, Coaching, Real Estate, Computer Consulting, are just a few. My editor, Cathy Wilson, works from her home. I found her on the Internet.

Be aware that some cities have ordinances about working from your home. Call your local city clerk to see what your community says about it. Check the web to find other ideas for a home business. There

are lots of opportunities if you are willing to work hard and stay with it. Do your homework. When you find a good one make sure you have the time and energy to follow through.

Spend less. Almost everyone can do that. About twelve years ago, Paul and I took a workshop about personal finances. It helped us get a grip on where our money was going. For thirty days we wrote down every-thing we spent. We included our monthly fixed expenses, like house and car payments. If there were payments due on a quarterly basis, like insurance, we divided that by three and included it in our total "outgo" for the month. Once we had that list, we put everything in categories. When we looked at this information, it was amazing to see where our money was going. For instance, we were spending about $1300 a year eating out on a regular basis at work. At about $5 or $10 per lunch it didn't seem like much, but when we totaled it for the year, we were shocked. We started taking our lunch when we could and used that money to pay down some debt.

Build a budget. There are a number of excellent authors who address personal finances. Our favorites include Ron Blue and Larry Burkett.

Both of them gave us some guidelines on how much we *"should"* be spending in each area. The amounts were all in percentages. For instance, Larry Burkett recommends that you spend no more than one third of your gross income on housing. That means that if we make $3000 per month, we should not spend more than $1000 per month on housing including tax, insurance and interest. We usually review our budget every year to see where we might have room for change. It has helped us keep our spending in line with our income. It has also helped be able to afford some of the luxuries.

Set aside some money for fun. Both Ron and Larry recommend setting aside some *"Fun Money."* This can be used for anything. Paul and I both have our own *"Fun Fund."* We give ourselves an allowance. If we don't spend it all, we put it in a savings account. I use mine to finance my adventures, like taking a class that is not necessary for my job or career but just interesting to me. That way, when I do something a little on the expensive side, it doesn't put a strain on the household budget. In fact, I enjoy it much more, because I don't feel guilty about using up the money we need to pay our bills. I also use this account to buy Paul gifts. I always felt funny buying him something using the household account.

Pay off high-interest debt. One of the best ways we found to improve our budget was getting rid of all high-interest debt. It can cost almost double for any item if you put it on a credit card and pay the minimum payment each month. That is why it is so easy to get credit today. The credit card companies want you to take a long time to pay off your bill.

> *"To have more money, you either have to
> make more or spend less."*

We have made it a habit to pay the credit card bill in full every month. One way we do that is by never charging anything that we cannot afford to pay for within 30 days. My sister-in-law, Coral, writes every charged purchase in her checkbook and subtracts it as though it were a check. That way she knows that she will have the money to pay the bill when it comes. It is also a good way to make sure all of the charges on your statement are correct. She balances her checkbook and her credit card statement at the same time.

Limit your spontaneous spending. Another reason that credit card companies like you to have credit cards is because you may end up spending more. It is harder to keep track of how much you spend when you use "plastic". Paul and I devised a way to minimize this by waiting 24 hours before buying anything that costs over $50, unless it is a necessity.

This is particularly important for me because I love to shop. I can go into any store and find something that I want to own. When I was a single mother, this used to get me into a lot of trouble. I got to the point of having to borrow money from my son's piggy bank to buy groceries.

For example, I would see a pair of shoes. If they were on sale and they fit and I liked them, I bought them. Even if an item is on sale, it is no bargain if you end up paying twice as much because of the interest. Now, I wait until I need something to even go shopping. It is a lot more frugal and a lot more fun. We have more money to do things like take our kids on a great vacation. And I have more room in my closet.

Getting rid of all your credit cards can help curb your spontaneous spending. Just cut them up. Make sure you call the credit card company and ask the best way to close the account. This is important. Not notifying them keeps your account open and on your credit report. You can also do this by using a debit card that deducts your purchase from your checking account automatically.

If you need credit cards for things like renting cars you can take all cards out of your wallet. Only put them back when you are going to use them that day. This also reduces the risk of having them lost or stolen.

Pay off long term debt. Once we got rid of all short-term debt, we started on long-term debt. We pay a little extra each month on our house payment. At the rate we are going, we will pay off our house about ten years early and save over $100,000 in interest. It is amazing what putting a little extra every month toward our mortgage will do to the payoff date. Most financial planners and accountants can figure it for you. There are even tools in some home finance programs for the computer. I use Quicken. The program calculates everything. Then we put in the extra payment we wanted to make. It gave us a report on when the loan would be paid off and how much total interest we would save.

What can you do to increase savings?

Americans, as a whole, are not very good a saving. Many of us are in debt because we have to use a credit card to pay for emergencies.

Start a regular savings plan. Even before you have your income under control either by spending less or making more, it is important to save. Many companies have savings and retirement plans. If that is not an option, then start a savings account. Our credit union will automatically deduct something from our paychecks every week if we choose that option. That way we don't have to remember to do it.

We make it a policy to pay ourselves first. Each week we put ten percent of our joint income in a saving's account. Once it is large enough to put into an investment, Paul moves it. We always keep some money there for emergencies. It is very reassuring to know that we can cover almost any unexpected expense. It also comes in handy if one of us has a particularly slow month. Another thing we have done is set up a fund that is easy to access with three months' "outgo." That way, if anything ever happened to either of us, we would have enough to live on for three months.

Start an investment plan. The bank or credit union is not the only place to increase your savings, but it is a good place to start. Paul is very good about investing. He reads and studies all of the options available to us on a regular basis. If you don't have time to do that, get a good financial planner.

Look for someone who will look out for your interests. A good financial planner will find out what you want to achieve and whether you are aggressive or conservative. It is important to invest regularly and for the long term. If you choose the right person, he/she can help you set up a system to achieve your financial goals.

Where and what do you want to give?

This may sound contrary to getting your finances in order but it is amazing—and not always logical—how this works. We decided to give at least ten percent of our income to some worthy charity. The more we gave the more we were blessed. We were not giving to get blessed but it always seemed to happen anyway. It did not always come back in the form of money. Once we were really struggling financially, our washer broke beyond repair. At the time we were not giving very much but we were still giving. Someone heard of our dilemma and sold us a brand new washer for about a quarter what we would have had to pay otherwise. We are still using that washer today.

Choose responsibly. We have chosen several places to give. The main one is our church. We chose the church because we agree with what they do with the money we give. They use about 30% of the total budget for helping others. We also like to give to groups that help youth. We even support some missionaries in a foreign country.

In addition, we recently became involved with *Grace Centers of Hope.* It is a program for people who need a hand. There are drug-addicts, battered women, and homeless people, all being helped. We support them because they don't believe in giving handouts. Their philosophy is "If you don't work, you don't eat." Every person who stays at the facility has to work. One person might cook, another might mop floors, but all must help if they want to stay or even just have a meal. The goal is to get people out of the center and on their own as soon as possible. This helps build self-respect.

Our philosophy is that it is our responsibility to give responsibly. We have been so fortunate that we want to give back. We have had to struggle. That was probably good for us. We want to support institutions and individuals that help the less fortunate get back on their feet. We had family and friends to help us. Not everyone is so blessed. But our main focus is to choose those organizations that "teach people how to fish instead of giving them a fish."

Volunteer. Perhaps you are not at the point of being able to contribute money. Volunteering your time is a great way to give. We have helped build a home for deaf orphans in a third world country, delivered gifts to children of prisoners during the holidays and served food to homeless people at a local soup kitchen. It is amazing how gratifying it was for us. Our children have even helped on occasion. They received a new understanding of how fortunate they were by comparison.

Give unneeded items. We live in a small home without much closet space or storage. Because of this we go through our closets every spring and package up anything that has not been used in the last twelve months. This includes clothes, household items non-perishable food and books.

We give this to the Salvation Army, Purple Heart and Grace Centers of Hope. They use it for their clients or put it in the resale shop. The resale shop is a great way for them to earn some much needed cash for operating expenses and it helps me immensely by eliminating unwanted clutter.

Make as much as you can. Save as much as you can. Give as much as you can. It is a philosophy that has served us well. You will benefit by adopting this philosophy and adapting it to your lifestyle.

Suggestions for Action this week:

1. Write down everything you spend for 30 days.
2. Total up what you spent in each category.
3. Determine your average monthly outgo.

4. Compare this to your average monthly income.
5. Pick some areas to cut back, save and pay down debt.
6. Find a good workbook about managing your finances.
7. Design and use a budget.
8. Set some money aside for fun.
9. Calculate what your spendable income would be if you eliminated your high interest debt.
10. Save at least 10% of your income. Pay yourself first.
11. Calculate what you would have in one year if you saved 10%.
12. Determine what percent you can give away and start doing that with your next paycheck.
13. Write about your progress in your journal.
14. Celebrate your success.

WEEK THIRTEEN

Analyze Your Itinerary

Most trips come with an itinerary. It is a good idea to review it before you leave on your journey. What does the itinerary for you life look like? What would you like it to look like? This week is about your values, purpose mission and vision. Analyze these and you will have the best itinerary for your life. The wonderful part is that you get to design your own.

There is an ancient book that says, *"Without a vision the people will perish."* I believe this with all my heart. A vision is about knowing where you will be in the future. It may be the most important thing in your life to know because it creates a reason for living.

One Friday morning a good friend of ours, Jess Livermore, came over to fish with Paul. Afterwards he stayed for lunch, so I joined them. During lunch, I asked Jess if he would read the manuscript for this book. He graciously agreed and asked me to tell him what it was about. When I told him that it was about change, he had a question. *"Is it okay if I don't want to change?"* That is a very important question because this book is really more about choice than it is change.

Jess had a choice. He decided that he liked his life just the way was. He has a great vision, mission, and purpose. He is very clear about what he values. He might not have them written down, but he has made his choice. You may be right where Jess is. If so, I applaud you. But even if you are, I suggest you read on. You may find a great deal of satisfaction in putting this all in writing.

In her best-selling book, *The Path,* Laurie Beth Jones writes in her introduction, *"My uncle once told me that during World War II, if an unidentified soldier appeared suddenly in the dark and could not state his mission, he was automatically shot without question. I wonder what would happen if we reinstituted that policy today."* I think it would elevate the importance of knowing our mission.

In the sixties, young people were asking, *"Why am I here?"* Knowing their vision, mission, purpose and clarifying their values would have given them the answer. If you have ever had a hard time making decisions, this chapter is for you. Knowing your vision, mission, purpose and values will greatly enhance your ability to make better choices for the right reasons. It is like having a custom designed itinerary at your fingertips. Be prepared. It may take a while but it is definitely worth it.

How do you define values/mission/purpose/vision?

Here are the definitions that I use for the following terms:

Values: These are less tangible but equally as important as vision, mission and purpose. In fact, they sometimes show up in your *"purpose"* statement. These are the things that are most important to you, like trust and love. Everyone has values. Most people just don't take the time to write them down. Other people will know what you value by the way you act. While you may have many values, it is best to narrow the list down to ten or twelve.

Mission: This is about what you want to do with your life. It should apply to every area of your life and will probably never change once you have determined the final version. It, however, can be refined as you learn and grow. Short and specific are the important things here.

Purpose: Here is the "Why." Why do you do what you do? Have you ever listened to the WII-FM? It is universal in its broadcast and everyone can hear it even if they never turn on their radios. It stands for

"What's *In It For Me*?" This may sound selfish, but it is much easier to do something that brings some value to your life. This should also be short and specific.

Vision: This is an overall picture of what you want your world to be like. It is not about you, but about your ideal view of the world, as you would design it. It needs to be less than twenty-five words so that you can easily remember it.

What do you value?

Following you will find a list of values. First, read through the list, adding any values that are not listed but may be important to you. Next, mark all the values that are important to you. Then, read only the ones you marked. Finally, narrow this list down to the top ten that are the most important and write them on a 3x5 card.

Acceptance	Connection	Forgiveness
Achievement	Contribution	Freedom
Admiration	Courage	Friendship
Adventure	Creativity	Fun
Affection	Curiosity	Generosity
Ambition	Decisiveness	Gratefulness
Appreciation	Dependability	Gratitude
Beauty	Determination	Growth
Care	Democracy	Happiness
Change	Enthusiasm	Helping
Choice	Ethics	Honesty
Comfort	Excitement	Honor
Communication	Excellence	Hope
Community	Expertise	Humor
Compassion	Faith	Independence
Competence	Fame	Influence
Cooperation	Fidelity	Integrity
Confidence	Focus	Intimacy

Involved	Privacy	Stability
Job Satisfaction	Productivity	Status
Joy	Purity	Tact
Kindness	Quality	Tenderness
Knowledge	Quiet	Tolerance
Leadership	Recognition	Thoroughness
Learning	Respect	Thoughtfulness
Loyalty	Reputation	Time Freedom
Love	Reward	Trust
Merit	Responsibility	Truth
Money	Romance	Understanding
Optimism	Security	Wealth
Organization	Serenity	Wisdom
Order	Self-respect	Winning
Passion	Sincerity	Wonder
Patience	Spontaneity	Work
Peace	Success	Zeal
Pleasure	Support	Other: _____
Power	Sophistication	Other: _____
Praise	Spirituality	Other: _____

How do you define your values?

Once you have narrowed down this list, write your definition for each of the top ten. A good way to start is by asking yourself the question, "*What does (insert value here) look like to me?*" Suppose I chose Romance as one of my top ten. What does "*romance*" look like to Linda? (Not "*What does romance look like to Paul?*") My answer: getting all dressed up and going out to dinner at a nice restaurant, making it long and leisurely with lots of conversation and hand holding.

> ## *"People will know what you value by the way you act."*

Why is it so important for me to define it? Because I may never have defined it before, yet complained that Paul did not give me any romance. He might think he has, but he has a different definition. His definition might be a quiet dinner at home watching a movie together.

While I might like that, too, it is not what I want when I ask for romance. If I ask for it and I don't define it for Paul, it is not his fault if I don't get what I want. Secondly, I am more likely to recognize it when I see it if I have what it looks like clear in my mind.

You might think that your values are important, but the principle of defining them is not. I believe that we get what we look for. Instead of complaining that you don't have any of these values in your life, go out and look for ways to discover and develop them. If you want more adventure in your life and the most exciting thing you do is change the channels on your television set, then guess what? You will probably not have much adventure. Once you define a value you will recognize it and experience it more often. You can make a conscious effort to add it to your life's experiences.

What do you want to do?

Pick a place and time when you will not be disturbed. This last piece of the process may take a while. Do not be deterred. Most really worthwhile things take time. You will need a pen, your journal and some time to reflect. There are some questions that will help you formulate your vision. This is not a test. There are no wrong answers. Relax and enjoy the process.

First question: *What would you be from "nine to five" if you didn't have to worry about how much money you made and were guaranteed success?* Write as much as you like. Allow yourself to dream. It might help to remember what it was like when you were very young and had not yet learned to put limitations on yourself. Keep writing until you can't think of anything else to write. If you have a hard time writing, then answer the question out loud and record it. If you don't like the idea of speaking into a tape recorder, then ask a friend to listen to your answer.

When I do this process with my clients, I take notes. When we are done, I read what I wrote back to them. I repeatedly ask, *"What else?"* until the answer is, *"Nothing else."* The point is to exhaust your thoughts and to think big. Don't worry about how you would accomplish what you are writing about. That will come later.

The next step involves reading what you (or your friend/coach) wrote. Read it aloud once through without stopping. Now read it again, noticing the verbs or action words. Notice the phrase that goes with each word. For example, *spend* is a verb but it doesn't tell the whole story. *"Spend time with my family"* does. Underline the action phrases as you go.

Once you have completed this step, turn to another page in your journal. Divide it into two columns. Write all of the underlined phrases in the first column. Label it *"Actions."* Look at this list and determine which words can apply to every area of your life. For instance, fishing is most often part of recreation and some people do it for a job. Either way, it is not related to *every* area of your life. However, you might have put *"enjoy my family and friends"* on your list. This could apply to every area of your life *and* you could go fishing as one way to fulfill this action.

What do I want to feel?

Now, review your answer to the question. *What would you be from "nine to five" if you didn't have to worry about how much money you made and were guaranteed success?* This time look for *feeling* words. Circle these words as you read. Copy the circled words into the second column of the second page. Title this column *"Feelings."* If you don't have anything to put in this column, don't be concerned. There is another step that will help you determine what to put here.

You now have two columns. One labeled *"Actions"* and one labeled *"Feeling."* You are ready to build your mission and purpose statement. Remember that your mission is what you want to do with your life. You may have several phrases in the *"Action"* column that can apply to every area of your life. At least one of these will be part of your mission. To choose, ask yourself these questions: *What is the most important to me? Which one is so important that I cannot imagine my life without it?* If you are having a hard time narrowing it down to one, then pick two but no more that three.

As you look at the list, you may notice that one phrase may encompass some of the others. This step is very important because it will be with you for the rest of your life. This is what you want to do with your life.

Example: In the action column you might have written: help others, enjoy life to the fullest, love my family, and spend time with my family. This could then be narrowed down to: *live life to the fullest and love my family.* Note that for you living life to the fullest would probably include helping others. And if you were loving your family you would probably be spending time with them. Therefore, your action statement (*live life to the fullest and love my family*) really encompasses all four statements.

Now ask yourself the following questions: *What would it feel like if everything I did would support living life to the fullest and loving my family? What would it be like if I could do all of what I just wrote, all of the time, and with great success?* Imagine that. See yourself being very successful living your mission. *What does it feel like?* Look at the column labeled *"Feelings."* If there is nothing there, then write the things you just imagined feeling. *What else would I feel?* Write it down. Keep asking, "What else?" Keep writing until the answer is *"Nothing else."*

Review the column of feelings. Which one is the most important for you to feel? If you can't narrow it down to one, then pick two. Your mission is *what* you want to do; your purpose is *why* you want to live it.

Example: The feeling column might have these words: peace, love, fulfillment and joy. That could be narrowed down to *joy and peace*. If you have joy and peace then you might also have fulfillment. Love is already part of the mission; therefore you will experience all four of the feelings you chose.

> *"Your mission is what you want to do; your purpose is why you want to do it!"*

Now it is time to put these two columns together. First, write your action phrases, then your feeling words. It will look something like this. "I want *to love my family* and *live life to the fullest* so I can have *joy and peace* in my life." Notice that the words in this statement were taken from the two columns on your second page. You simply narrowed the list down to the ones that were most important. The first part is the mission and the second part is your purpose.

Another way to say it is: *My mission is to love my family and live life to the fullest in order to achieve my purpose of living a joyful and peaceful life.* Here is another example of a mission and purpose statement: *My mission is to serve God, love my family and inspire others to greatness for the purpose of experiencing joy and fulfillment in my life.*

It is important that this mission and purpose statement be yours. The thought of living a life that is described by your statement should make you smile. It is part of what makes life worth living.

What do you want your life to be?

I had never really distinguished between a mission statement and a vision statement until I met my coach, Barry Demp. He helped me see that creating a vision of what I want my world to be like would help me move toward it. After a lot of thought and preparation, I did what he asked me to do: *"Imagine that you have achieved the results in your life that you deeply desire. Use the present tense to describe the accomplishments you envision for these areas."* He gave me seven areas to consider. I would ask you to use the eight areas from the *"Balance Wheel."* They are: Financial, Professional, Physical, Recreational, Emotional, Mental, Spiritual, Relational.

Write it in present tense. For example, for my career, I wrote: *" I am a Certified Master Coach, with a full practice."* I did not write, *"Someday I will be a Certified Master Coach with a full practice."* I wrote it as if it had already happened. It was not true on the date that I wrote it, but it was my vision of the future for me. It is now a reality.

Once you have a statement related to each of the eight areas from the *"Balance Wheel,"* you are ready to build your vision. Start by reviewing your values and mission/purpose statement. The mission/purpose statement is about you. The vision statement is *not* about you. It is a picture of the future written in present tense that *includes* you. It should be short enough to remember but long enough to include what is most important to you. The more powerful the statement the more value it will be to you. Use descriptive words that inspire and encourage. Your vision statement needs to evoke emotion in you. When you read it, you should be inspired.

Start by answering the following question. *What would your perfect world look like?* Dream big. A big vision will bring big results. Make it clear. That way you will recognize it when you see it. This may take some time. Don't give up. There are companies that take years to create a vision statement. Review what you have written about values, mission and purpose. With that in mind begin with *"My personal life vision is…"*

> *"A big vision will bring big results!"*

Examples: *"My personal life vision is a world that values children and honors the family."* *"My personal life vision is a courageous, creative and passionate world full of joy and beauty where all people support and encourage each other and celebrate life."* The important thing to remember is that your vision statement is something to aspire to while you are living the life you love.

We do not live in a perfect world, but you and I can be part of making it better. You can make it better for yourself and everyone around you by looking for ways to live your life according to your values, mission, purpose and vision. It is amazing to see the opportunities that will arise for you to live the life you love.

Suggestions for Action this week:

1. Write/print your purpose/mission statement, values, and life vision statement on large index cards.
2. Post them where you will read them every day.
3. Make a smaller version of each one and carry them with you.
4. Refine or redefine them at the end of each thirteen-week process.
5. Consider them when making decisions.
6. Make a list in your journal of ways for you to incorporate them into your daily life. Make note of how and when you do so.
7. Live your life so that people will recognize you by your statements and your values.

EPILOGUE

I am sitting at my computer. I am writing the last page of this book. It is September 11, 2001. No doubt you remember this date. It is the day that hijacked commercial airplanes crashed into the World Trade Center, Pentagon and a field in Pennsylvania. I keep thinking, *"What can I do?"* In spite of the tragedy, we as individuals have a choice. We as a *country* have a choice. We can choose to become victims. We can choose to become vengeful. We can choose to take a stand. We can choose to be thankful…no, not for the tragedy, but that we live in a free country. But freedom comes with a price. Change has chosen us, Americans. What have *you* done since September 11, 2001 to change your life?

Notes:

NOTES:

WHAT IS A COACH?

(First published in Coach to Coach Newsletter John G. Agno, Newsletter Editor & Business Coach johnagno@signatureseries.com Voice: 734.426.2000 Fax: 734.426.2109)

When you hear the word coach, do you think of your favorite sports team? Well, there is a fairly new profession out there: life coach, job coach, change coach or success coach are some of the names for it. According to an article in *Harvard Management Update* (January 1999), some people seem to think of coaching and managing as the same thing.

"But coaching isn't mystical; it isn't even hard to learn. In fact all that may be necessary is to rid yourself of some common misconceptions." This article debunks several myths about coaching.

Myth # 1: Nobody can really define coaching.
Fact: Coaching is a well-defined process, with start points and end points. The heart of the process lies in a person's potential, and that's not always easy to quantify.

Myth #2: Coaching is managing with a happy face.
Fact: Making sure someone achieves certain performance levels is managing. Helping them handle problems for themselves is coaching.

Myth #3: Coaching is just another name for mentoring.
Fact: A coach is more dispassionate than a mentor. If someone fails to live up to a commitment, a mentor might say, "You're disappointing

me." Coaches say; "This is what you said you wanted, and you're not doing it."

Myth #4: Being a coach means being a cheerleader.
Fact: A coach doesn't just praise an individual's efforts. A coach helps people understand what they need to change in order to attain their professional goal.

Myth 5: Coaching takes a lot of time.
Fact: Coaching relationships can last anywhere from three months to two years, depending on what the coachee is trying to accomplish. But during that period it should take at most 30-55 minutes per week. That's the time you spend checking on what someone has done since you last spoke and helping him/her figure out what steps to take next.

Myth #6: Coaching is a kind of psychotherapy.
Fact: Coaches, like all businesspeople, need to have a grasp of psychology, to help understand what motivates people. But coaching focuses on what to do now, not on what went wrong in the past.

Myth #7: One recipe can handle all coaching situations.
Fact: There is not a "one size fits all" approach to coaching. Individuals and their goals are different, and so is what each person needs to learn to achieve them.

Myth #8: Some people just can't be coached.
Fact: If an individual is truly receptive to coaching and it still isn't working, there may be problems with the relationship or the coach's style. Finding a different coach may bring better results.

Myth #9: If you successfully coach people they may leave their jobs.
Fact: While some employee who achieves new goals will leave, far more will feel greater loyalty to an organization that is interested in their professional development.

Myth #10: Coaching does not add to a company's bottom line.
Fact: Coaching can have a positive impact on performance, but it is not a short-term process. Coaching prospects should be people you think can be even greater assets to the organization than they already are.

(For a full reprint of this article, see Harvard University, Harvard Management Update, by von Hoffman, Keyword: Coach on the Internet)

Obviously, von Hoffman is talking about coaches within an organization. But in the United States today, as many as 10,000 independent coaches make their living coaching clients outside the client's company. People pay coaches anywhere from $250 to $3000 per month; these people might include entrepreneurs, headhunters, vice presidents of major corporations, and young executives. Some people want to lose weight, quit smoking or just learn to balance their personal and business life. One woman increased her income from $65K to $300K in less than a year with the help of a coach. When surveyed by Coach University, 70% of clients using such independent coaches were very satisfied and 28% were satisfied with the results.
Do you think you might want to hire a coach? Here's what you should remember:

1. *Interview your potential coach before you commit, and ask some hard questions.*
    Most coaches require payment up front by the month, so be sure you want to spend at least three months working with this person before you send them any money. Most coaches start with at least

a three-month commitment. This is based on the premise that it takes at least 90 days to affect a lasting change.

2. *Most coaching is done on the phone or over the Internet.*
    Are you comfortable on the phone? Do you like to communicate through e-mail? This seems to fit in today's busy lifestyle, but it might not be for you.

3. *Coaches hold people accountable.*
    Are you ready for that? Coaches tend to ask the hard questions that we are not willing to ask ourselves.

4. *Ask for referrals and credentials.*
    And call the referrals. Anyone can post testimonials on a website.

5. *Don't expect the coach to be an expert in your field.*
    Some coaches specialize in an area, but most coaches consider you the expert. His/her job is to help you find the answer. If you want an expert, look for a consultant instead and be willing to pay three to five times more per hour.

6. *If money is an issue, consider using a "budding" coach.*
    Most are anxious to have paying clients no matter how small the fee. Here are two places you look to find referral services: www.coachville.com and www.coachtrainer.com. Call some of the coaching schools and ask for a coach in training: AAA Coaching Partners, B-Coach, Coach U, Coach Trainer. There are others. Look them up on the Internet.

7. *Make sure your coach has a goal to stop being your coach.*
    A good coach wants to get you working on your own. However, most coaches will make themselves available intermittently to former

clients for a short phone call or e-mail for up to a year after the regular meetings have stopped. There may be an additional fee for this but it usually does not require a long-term commitment.

8. *Be sure to do what you say you will do between meetings.*
    You will be wasting your money if you don't follow through on your commitments. One advantage of having a coach is that you will get more done in the same amount of time. If you are not completing your action steps then why are you spending your time and money to work with a coach?

9. *Tell your coach what you want, what is working now and what is not working.* He/she needs that information to help set up a plan for you to reach your goal/s. Coaches are not mind readers. If you need more of something then ask for it. It will help you work together better and you will, more likely, get what you need.

10. *Set high standards and expectations.*
    If you aim low that is what you will get. Also, if you could do it on your own you wouldn't need a coach. So pick some lofty goals, something that will stretch you.

FAMOUS PEOPLE WHO
HAVE CHOSEN CHANGE

Here is a list of some famous people whose lives are inspiring. Take some time to research their stories. You may be surprised with what you find.

Roger Bannister—The first man to run the four-minute mile in spite of the fact that he was told that he could die if he continued to pursue this goal.

Rush Limbaugh—He was told that he would never make it in radio, yet he has the largest listening audience in the United States in spite of the controversial nature of his show.

Dave Pelzer—The most abused child in California history, he has gone on to help others with similar backgrounds and has written three best selling books on the subject.

Christopher Reeve—A world-renowned actor who survived a riding accident, and became a quadriplegic, he has returned to acting and become a director.

John Stossel—A misfit as a young boy plagued by stuttering and tormented by the other kids at school, he overcame these roadblocks to become one of the leading ABC anchors.

Barbara Walters—A pioneer in the field of broadcast journalism, rejected by major networks early in her career, she pursued her dream and became one of the first woman to reach the number one position with a major network.

Oprah Winfrey—In spite of a tragic childhood, she went on to become a "household word", an entrepreneur, and the number one talk show host in America.

Zig Ziglar—From humble beginnings and several failures, he has become one of the most well known and respected speakers in the world.

Stories About Change

Laurie Lynne Limbers
Harness Racing

It wasn't really a conscious choice for me to train and race. When I was young I always wanted to be a jockey but since I didn't grow up around horses I really didn't have the background for it. Being 5' 9' and a woman didn't help either. As you may know, jockeys are usually men and very short. I just knew that some day I would have horses.

Eventually, Mike and I purchased enough property that we could have some riding horses. The area that we live is big into harness racing. There are a lot of small farm tracks nearby, so I went to work for a trainer cleaning stalls and jogging horses. It was pretty dirty work but I loved being around the horses. A couple months later I was driving in my first matinee fair race. Since size doesn't really matter for a harness driver I knew this is what I was meant to do. It wasn't easy. To drive at the major racetracks, you have to work your way up the ladder, as with most everything.

First, I had to get a license to drive at matinees, which are races at county fair tracks where there is no betting. The prize is having your picture taken and a new horse blanket. After doing that for a while, the USTA (United States Trotting Association) requires drivers to get signatures from other trainers and drivers who think you are qualified to get a "Q" license. This happened for me in 1987. I could then drive in races at county fairs and qualifying races where betting is done (A qualifying race is a race held once a week to determine whether or not a horse is fast enough). It takes a lot of driving at these races to qualify for the next level, a "P" license (Provisional license). After driving for about a year or more with a "P" license, you can approach the stewards at the tracks for your "A" license. As long as you have been a safe driver you will get your "A" license. That is where I am now.

I'm first considered a "Trainer"; a horse can't race unless the owner of the horse has a trainer. People hire me to train and race their horse. I am responsible for keeping it fit, shod, and fed. I enter the horse in a race. Then I take the horse to the track and race it. This involves harnessing it, and warming it up. If I'm driving it I will do that, too. After the race, I undress him and give him a bath and cool him down. A trainer has to be licensed by the USTA. I am also called a "Driver." I usually drive the horses that I own or the ones that I train for other people.

I love the speed of sitting behind a powerful animal that loves what he is doing as much as I do. The adrenaline is very addictive. I love going out early in the morning when the sun is just rising. It's just me and my horse jogging on the track. It's different everyday. Sometimes I'll see the fog rising or the first snow falling. Once when I was on this little track in the middle of some woods, I got out on the track and it was full of snakes sunning themselves. The horse didn't seem to even notice.

I am still in awe every time I go to the Northville Track for winter races. When I go into the paddocks I can see the steam rising off of the horses that have been warmed up. They are all standing there in "full battle armor" waiting with their blankets on, keeping their muscles warm. They're blowing steam from their nostrils. Some are standing so quietly, as if they have to save their energy for the race. Then there are the ones that can't contain themselves. They are pawing at the floor and kicking the walls. They can be pretty rough on the groom that is taking care of them. It's almost too much for them to wait.

There is just so much to love. I own a yearling that I am breaking right now. I love that she has put all of her trust in me to teach her the right things to do. I love the soft part of a horse's nose and just the smell of them. I just love the sounds they make when I walk by their stalls. I can hear them talking to me.

Even with all of the things I love, there are things that make it difficult. I don't like the late nights racing in the winter. Sometimes I leave for the track in the dark and come home in the early morning hours. I have to bring my horse back to the barn and it might be –10 0 .I have to make sure that my horse is taken care of before I can head home. Jogging horses on really cold days isn't too much fun either. Sometimes my fingers freeze in the first mile with four miles to go. Another thing that is really hard for me is when I have raised a horse to become a racehorse but he just doesn't have what it takes. I can't keep them all but I want to.

It's hard to explain what I do. People don't understand that I can't just take a day off or not go to the barn for one day. It is a seven-day per week job with no holidays or paid vacations. Sometimes it seems fanatical but it really isn't. I am in charge of living creatures that live in stalls with no way to forage for themselves. I have their lives in my hands. This is the choice I've made. I have to follow through with all that goes with it.

I'm really not a loud boisterous person. I would say I am more on the shy side. Because of my career as a driver I have to go out and drive against men and in front of thousands of people. These races are simulcast across the country. Sometimes that is difficult for me if I let myself think about it too much, but I guess that is part of the thrill. The most exciting event is the winner's circle. People that I don't know are cheering and congratulating me. I don't think that I will ever become complacent about that.

Recently, the Michigan Breeders Association put together a calendar to earn money for "EPM" research. (EPM is a parasite that attacks the horse's nervous system. It is very devastating and money is needed for research to develop a vaccine.) They decided to put a driver on each page. Being the only woman driver out there right now I was asked to pose for one of the months. I figured I had to do it. It was a lot of fun; I actually had to sign autographs. It was kind of strange going to the races and seeing my picture everywhere advertising the calendar.

In spite of how it may seem, I really am a very normal person with a normal family. I love to shop and eat and go to the movies or just stay home. I don't always have to be around horses. In fact I really enjoy the time that I have when I'm not around them. Mike and I have recently gotten into sea kayaking. It's very relaxing and a great way to unwind. Racing is like any other job; sometimes it's good just to be doing something else. When I look at a horse I see work!

This is pretty much a male dominated profession. I can't really say for sure how many women there are in this field but I am usually the only one racing in a night program. There were a few in Michigan that have driven in the past but not anymore. Women seem to get to the pari mutual tracks and then just fade away. There is a lot of pressure out there. There are women across the country and around the world that drive but they are few and far between. It is very competitive. There was one woman during 60's and 70's named Bea Farber that was quite famous. I can't say that there has been anyone like her since.

One of the toughest things about being a woman in this sport is that everyone is always watching, waiting for me to mess up. For example, early in my career, I would drive anything just to get the track time. There was a big black mare that had a bad reputation for being quite mean called Rocktime Terry. I agreed to drive her even though more experienced drivers wouldn't. We came out of the paddock and onto the track to parade in front of the grandstands. She decided to rear up so I tapped her with the whip. She came back down and kicked both feet at me. She proceeded to do this to me until we got right in front of everyone. Then she really let me have it and flipped me out of the bike onto the track. There I am on the ground and she is trying to back up over me. My driving line was wrapped around my foot. Luckily, as she backed up I got the lines off of my leg and climbed away from her. She proceeded to race around the track alone. After she went the usual mile, off the track she came. Needless to say she is pulling an Amish buggy right now.

Considering how dangerous this sport is, I've been very fortunate. I have never had anything more that a sprained ankle or a few bumps and cuts from being kicked. Some of my friends haven't been so lucky. Recently one broke both of his arms and about 8 years ago another friend was killed in a race.

Even though I love what I do I have some advice for people who want to do something unusual for a career. Make sure that it is really something that you want to do. Is it worth the sacrifices that you WILL have to make? If it is, don't let other people discourage you. It's usually because it might be inconvenient for them. Or they might be a little jealous. But don't forget about the rest of your life. Keep as much of that in tact as possible. You will need some normalcy in your life. And mainly, if you are a woman going into something that is typically a man's profession don't whine and moan that your aren't being treated fairly. Never think you know it all. No respect will be gained from that. Just stick it out until they know you are there to do a job just like they are. Surprisingly it will all come together.

Dan Miller
Career Coach

I was raised on a dairy farm in rural Ohio. My father, besides being a farmer, was also the pastor of the Mennonite church in our one-traffic-light town. This interesting combination gave me a unique perspective on the world. I was not allowed to join in with many of the activities of the other kids in town. Going to ball games, swimming pool, proms, dances and free time was out. Fancy cars, TV's, current fashions and other "worldly" possessions were absolutely forbidden. Yet in that environment, nothing could stop my mind from wandering. Out in the fields, I imagined a world I had never seen. I wanted to do more, go more, have more and be more than anything I was seeing.

Somehow, in that protected world, when I was about ten years old, I was able to get a copy of the little 45-rpm record by Earl Nightingale titled *The Strangest Secret*. Here I heard this gravelly-voiced man say that I could be more and do more by simply changing my thinking. He talked about six words that could change your life! *We become what we think about*. What I could conceive I could achieve. Knowing this radical way of thinking would not be welcome in my house, I hid that little record under my mattress, bringing it out night after night to hear again the promises of a better life. While my peers were hiding their girlie magazines under their beds, this was the message of hope and opportunity that captured my imagination.

I began to see the impact of that thinking creeping into my belief system. I would take the lawn mower engine apart to see if I could improve its power and efficiency. I salvaged items from the local dump and would improvise new machines and inventions. We lived miles out in the country and it was impossible to get to town on my own to see my buddies. So I connected a contraption behind our small tractor. It was an old rear end from a car. By attaching the driveshaft to the power take off (PTO) on the tractor, I was able to take the tractor out of gear and have a drive mechanism that would push the tractor much faster than it was ever intended to go. Once I found an old Indian motorcycle in an abandoned house and tried for weeks to get it running. I sold Christmas cards to all the neighbors and dreamed of winning the grand prize. After my mother canned all the sweet corn our cellars would hold, I would get up at 5:30 in the morning, go out and pick the remaining corn and head for the main road with our little tractor and a trailer full of excess corn. With my homemade sign, I would sell corn for $.30 a dozen and collect my growing nest egg.

My first car was entirely handmade. I purchased a 1931 Model A Ford for $50. Slowly and meticulously, I put together a running street rod. When I had five dollars, I would go to the junkyard and buy a generator or a set of seats. I learned by doing, listening and talking to anyone who knew more than I did. While my friends conned their parents into buying them their first cars, I methodically put in every spare minute in that unheated old chicken coop where I was building my car. Approximately one year later, I drove out with an eye stopping "hot rod." It had an exposed Chrysler "hemi"' connected to a Packard transmission, followed by an Olds rear end that had been welded solid for constant "posi-traction". My innovative thinking and efforts were beginning to pay off. The farming environment was giving me exposure to multiple opportunities to learn and experiment. What I could conceive I really could achieve.

Upon completing high school, I was expected to become a full time part of our family farming operation. But I wanted more and I knew that college would help open new doors of opportunity for me. I was required to help with the duties of dairy and farming chores beginning at 5:30 AM. So I enrolled in a branch campus of Ohio State University where I could attend from 6:00 PM-10:00 PM. Being a poor farm kid but with good grades, I qualified for the help to get me through college. Before beginning my freshman year, I received an $1800 grant for tuition. However, my entrepreneurial stirrings were already blasting away in my mind. There was $1800 sitting in my bank amount and the tuition would be due over a period of the next several months.

Surely, I could leverage that money into something more. I responded to an ad in a magazine much like many of you have seen. *"Get into the vending business; you don't have to do anything. We install the machines. All you have to do is collect the money."* My 1800 purchased ten hot cashew machines. What could be more appealing than cashews under heat? This was going to be too easy. Yes, a representative from the company did come to place the machines. His center of comfort was obviously in the sleaziest bars he could find. Here I was a shy, backward Mennonite Kid and he was placing my machines in places I had never been allowed to set foot. I discovered something very quickly. Guess what happens to cashews under heat if they are not stirred about every 12 hours? They MOLD! I immediately began getting calls from these fine establishments telling me to get those machines out of there or suffer the wrath of their inebriated customers. I picked up my ten precious machines and hid them in an old storage shed. Months later I sold them for roughly $.10 on the dollar. When the tuition came due, I had to get out and hustle for the money I had lost.

Through the college years, I bought old cars, fixed them up and sold them to other students. I also tried Amway, Erase Dirt, and a host of other network marketing companies. I looked at business opportunities and watched the growing popularity of franchises. Years later, I started a recreational vehicle rental business. Then I opened an auto accessories business where we focused on the needs of the new car dealers. After selling that business to a couple of the employees, I bought a health and fitness center. I personally don't like the fitness center environment. I am much too impatient for the socializing and slow pace of the workout process in that setting. But I saw the bottom line and knew I could make money. After three frustrating years, I sold that business at public auction, taking about a $430,000 loss.

I have built service businesses, provided consulting, speaking and public seminars. Currently Joanne, my patient, supportive wife of 31 years, and I provide executive career coaching, host a popular radio show called *Career Link* and develop innovative personal improvement products for mail order marketing.* Our lives are streamlined and focused. We have more control of our time than we had imagined was possible. Our children and grandchildren live within minutes of our home and we spend many hours together each week. I enjoy the feedback of other people who have benefited from our efforts and consider ourselves to be truly blessed with the multiple characteristics of true success. I hope you can bypass some of the lessons I learned from the school of hard knocks and can experience the absolute joy that I have had in having a creative plan come together.

Lagniappe

(Pronounced lan' yap, this is Cajun French for "a little something extra")

My story

As you read this book, you learned about some of the changes I made in my life. I want you to know the rest of the story. If I didn't tell you the whole story, you would not really know who I am. I grew up in a family with a mother and father and three siblings. We were by all accounts the typical American family of my generation.

Mom stayed at home until my younger brother was in school. My dad owned his own business—several, in fact. When I was small, he was a partner in a tire store. Going there as a little girl, I remember being told to be very careful not to get dirty. When I was a little older, Dad bought a "service station," a different thing entirely from a gas station today. There they made repairs, changed oil, pumped gas and washed your car for you. My brothers both worked there. We have home movies of my little brother at age six or seven pumping gas and helping out at the station. The girls weren't allowed to work there. At the time, that was considered man's work.

When I was about four or five years old, my older sister, Joyce, went to New York to be a model, but she didn't stay long. She missed her boyfriend too much. After a few months, she came home, got married and started having kids. Her husband went to college on a football scholarship, played pro ball in Canada for a while and then went into the oil business. They are still married and live in Canada, as do all their children. They had seven children, although one died tragically at the age of two from a rare heart condition.

My older brother, Dale, joined the Marines when I was about 13. I was so mad at him for going away; I wouldn't even talk to him when he called home! He was stationed in New Zealand for part of his tour, where he met a wonderful girl, whom he married. They came to live in our hometown and had five children. Dale had his own water purification business. He never really achieved what he wanted with that before he died in 1996, but his oldest son is doing really well with it now. Everyone keeps saying, "If only Dad were here to see how the business is doing."

My younger brother, Mike, lives near me now in southeast Michigan. He came for a visit one summer and fell in love with a local girl. They got married and now have two sons. They have done a number of unique things to earn a living. Right now my brother makes an excellent living in the auto body repair business and his wife trains harness race horses.

Before I was fourteen I had a pretty uneventful life. Up until then, I had gone to a parochial school—with the same kids—for eight years. Then I went to high school, the first time I was around people of different faiths. I was what most people would have called a "goody two shoes." In high school, I made friends easily but did not quite make it into the "in crowd." I was always acutely aware of this, though I tried not to let it show. Somehow I never quite made it to the top, never quite won anything. For example, I was selected to be in the school beauty pageant but didn't win any awards. I was chosen as an *alternate* for Girl's State. In the Junior Miss Pageant, I came in as first runner up. No matter what I tried, I was always second best. To tell the truth, many other girls would have probably given their eyeteeth to even be in the running, but I was always disappointed about not being number one. I certainly wanted to come in first.

I went right into college after graduating from high school to Louisiana State University in Baton Rouge, right in my hometown. Like most of the girls my age, I joined a sorority. My "big sister" introduced me to the man I would marry. We started dating in 1966 and, because he was in a fraternity, we got "dropped" (or lavaliered, depending on what part of the country you come from). A year later we got "pinned." He was, by now, president of his fraternity. I never admitted it to anyone, but I really had my heart set on being fraternity Sweetheart that year. After all, the sweetheart of the president was *always* elected sweetheart of the fraternity.

I remember so well the night just before the big dance where they would announce the sweetheart and her court. My boyfriend said he needed to talk to me. We were alone and he looked very serious. He said that it was very difficult for him to tell me, but I was not elected sweetheart of the fraternity. I thanked him for telling me and said it was okay. In fact, I ended up comforting him. To be honest, I felt fine about it because I didn't believe him. I thought he was saying that because he wanted me to be surprised. But he was telling me the truth. When I came in first runner-up, I had to act like it didn't bother me. I couldn't even go to him for comfort. I am fifty-three years old now and I have never told anyone how badly I was hurt that night. I guess God and I were the only ones who ever knew how unhappy I was that I didn't win.

I graduated in January 1969 with a degree in elementary education and started teaching right away. We were married that summer. I was 21 years old. My new husband was accepted into medical school and we moved 500 miles away. I had never lived anywhere but my hometown. Outwardly, I made the change just fine, but inside I was dying. Although I wouldn't have admitted it, I was still very inexperienced in relationships.

Because I didn't feel happy, I began to look for something to fill the gap. I threw myself into the woman's organization of the Student AMA and ran almost every committee at one time or another. This was the early 1970's and everyone was doing their "own thing." I remember vividly the first time I went out in public without a bra. It was a party with all our friends—my husband's classmates and their spouses. I felt like everyone was staring at me.

I realized that committee work and burning my bra would not "fulfill" me so I decided I wanted a baby. My husband was a senior in medical school by this time, and we had been married for almost four years. Although I would never recommend that anyone have a baby just because it was the "right time," this was the best thing we ever did.

As much as I loved my new son, I was still not fulfilled. I was still searching, as were most people under 30. Because of my feelings of dissatisfaction, my husband and I started seeing a marriage counselor. She was great and seemed to understand my dilemma. The dilemma: I was married to an "up and coming" doctor; I had a good teaching job; my son was healthy, smart and adorable; but I wasn't happy. My husband, on the other hand, was happy. He just didn't understand what was wrong with me, but our therapist did. Then she quit. I don't remember why she left her practice, but when she did, it devastated me. She turned us over to a very competent colleague, but it was never the same. I felt so alone.

The summer after my son turned a year old, I went to a family wedding out of state. This was the first time I had ever left my husband alone to care for our son for more than a few hours. My cousin's husband-to-be had a single brother that stood up in the wedding alongside me. If this were a cheap romance novel, the next thing you'd read would be, "and their eyes met..."

Within three weeks of this wedding, I had left my husband of five years and moved more than a thousand miles further from my family. I didn't know anyone within two hundred miles. I eventually divorced my husband and began living with this man. We were married as soon as my divorce was final. It would probably not surprise you that three years later, this new husband, had an affair with someone I thought was my friend. To top it off, everyone else knew. In order to show him that two could play this game, I had a very short-lived affair with someone we both knew. I feel most sorry about this part of the story. I just used this wonderful man to get back at my second husband for humiliating me. Our divorce was final in March. The following July, we would have been together for five years.

In spite of pleas from my family, I stayed in Michigan. I began life as a single parent, angry and bitter, without hope for recovery. After all, who would ever want me? I was a two-time loser. I began a journey into self-destruction. I partied, I ran around, I drank and smoked.

I had a job as a teacher but at the time, we were paid bi-weekly for nine months. Since I hadn't planned on being single, I did not really save anything to live on during the summer. I had to find something to support my son and myself. I took a job as a waitress in a small public golf club restaurant. That was an adjustment. I had never waited tables before. I gained a new appreciation for wait staff.

Even though I had been married to two different people, I had not been single for over ten years. I wasn't sure about dating. Teaching didn't offer much in the way of a social life. Some friends told me about a singles organization that sounded really interesting. I went with a girlfriend the first time and immediately got involved.

I volunteered to chair one of the events. Eventually, I was on the planning board where I served for several years. While I was there, I met some very interesting people, some of whom I am still friends with today. In fact, I ended up working for one of the other people on the board, Mike Wickett. He is the person who introduced me to speaking and training.

Mike recommended that I take the Dale Carnegie Sales Course. I won the sales talk semi-finals. As a result, I went out with some other members of the class to celebrate. I was sitting across from one of the graduate assistants named Jim who was talking with the person next to me about God. I thought, *"What a strange thing to be talking about in a bar!"* But he had my interest.

I overheard Jim say something about *"Born Again."* That phrase really stuck out for me. So I asked Jim what it meant. Jim told me that God had sent his son, Jesus, to die on the cross for my sins. I already knew that. He said that Jesus had risen three days later and was seated at the right hand of his father in heaven. I already knew that. *"So what does that have to do with being "Born Again?"* What he said next made me think. He asked me if I wanted to go to heaven. *"Of course,"* I said.

"Do you want to know for sure?"

"Yes!"

"Then accept the gift God has given you."

"What gift?"

"The gift of love that he gave you when he gave up his son to pay the price for your sins." He went on to tell me that restitution must be made for every sin and God offered his son for restitution. He said that if I admitted that I had sinned and was willing to accept Jesus' death as restitution for my sins then I would be *"Born Again"* into the family of God as a totally new person.

Jim said, *"That is what being 'Born Again' means. Then you will know for sure where you will go when you die."*

"But why would he do that for me?"

"Because he loves you. And because nothing you could ever do would be good enough to earn heaven or pay for your sins."

"How do I accept the gift?"

"Just tell God that you accept the gift."

I really believed that God loved me. I just couldn't accept the fact that he would let me off the hook so easily. I always thought I had to earn heaven. What about the sins that I would commit in the future? Did this mean I could do anything I wanted to do because Jesus paid for my sins? I still had a lot of questions but that was enough talk about God for one night. I excused myself and drove home in deep thought.

Could this be true? Could it be this easy? I couldn't stop thinking about it. Why couldn't I shrug this off like I had so many times before? I was a good person. I tried to do the right thing. No, I wasn't perfect but who was? What was happening to me? God was becoming a pest. I felt like he was tapping on my shoulder and he wasn't going to quit until I answered him.

"Okay, you win! I have no idea what this all means or if it is even true but I want to know for sure that I am going to heaven. I want this gift. It sounds pretty selfish to me but if you are offering it, then I am accepting it." And I started to cry. It was one of those shoulder-shaking sobs that just wouldn't stop. It was almost as if I was being bathed in tears. When I stopped, I felt clean.

The next week is a blur. I just know that I couldn't wait to tell Jim. He was shocked. He took me to the instructor, Pat Conner, so I could tell him what had happened. He was excited and invited me to go to church with him and his wife. I accepted. They took me to Ward Presbyterian Church the following Sunday. That was December 22, 1981 and I have been there every Sunday since unless I was sick or out of town.

I have grown so much since then. I became very involved with Single Pointe. True to form, I joined every group and ended up being in charge of many of the committees. Timm Jackson was the pastor then. He and his wife Karen helped me so much. Karen spent time with me teaching me what it meant to be a child of God. She was like my spiritual coach. She helped me though more than one struggle. She and Timm moved to Arizona but we still stay in touch.

In 1985, I attended my 20th high school reunion. I had never attended any of the previous reunions. I was so excited about seeing all of my classmates. It was a three-day event. On Friday night we had a "sock hop" at the school gym. When I walked in, I saw two of my old friends and we hugged like we had never lost touch. It was like that all evening long.

The next evening was a dinner dance. That is where Paul and I connected. We hit it off right away. We decided to take a walk. As we walked and talked we got to know each other again. At some point Paul said something to me that I will never forget. *"You are very different than any of the women I have met since my wife and I split up. What makes you so different?"*

I will never forget my answer, either. *"I am not sure what you think makes me so different but whatever you think it is, I bet it is not what you think. If you really want to know I will tell you."* He said that he did and then I said, *"I am a 'Born Again' Christian."*

"Christians don't look like you!"

I laughed, *"What are Christians supposed to look like?"*

"Oh, I don't know. I guess I just think about the ones that wear such ugly clothes and go away to the mission field to convert the heathens."

"Well, I am a Christian and that is the most important thing you will ever know about me."

It turned out that Paul had been a Christian since he was twelve years old. He had just not been doing much in the way of showing it in the last twenty-six years. After that night, he started going to church with his mom every Sunday. We started a long distance romance and were married within the year.

I believe that God orchestrated and blessed this marriage. He continues to do that every day. We are more in love today than we were the day of the wedding. We continue to grow. It is not always easy. We are still human. But, as Paul said once when a friend of mine asked him why he thought that our marriage would last (given our past history), *"Christ is the center of our relationship. In the past neither of us had that. Now we do."*

I can remember saying that my life was like a jigsaw puzzle. When I poured all the pieces out on the table it looked like a mess. I had managed to put it together. It looked pretty good. There were a few cracks but for the most part it was put together skillfully with a lot of hard work on my part (at least that is what *I* thought). The only problem was that there was one piece missing right in the middle of the blue sky. I couldn't find it anywhere. I thought it was lost for good. I tried to put other things in its place (career, business, partying) but nothing really fit. Once I had that conversation with God on the way home from the Dale Carnegie class, I knew what had been missing all along. It was God. Now the puzzle is complete. I can still see the lines between the pieces. Every once in a while, something or someone bumps the table and things get a little messed up. Some of the pieces have even fallen on the floor. The difference now is that *God* puts them back. And for some reason when he puts them back, they fit better. I can hardly see the lines any more.

You may be someone who doesn't even believe in God. If so, this might seem like a ridiculous story. Maybe you do believe in God and think you have to earn heaven. If so, it probably still seems like a ridiculous story. All I know is that this is what happened to me and my life has never been the same. Sure, I make mistakes. I still have to work hard to be good. The difference is that I am not trying to earn heaven. I want to be good because I appreciate the sacrifice that Jesus made for me. I am not perfect, just forgiven. I am still learning and growing. This is the main reason I wrote *Choose Change…before Change Chooses You*. Many people wait until their lives are in shambles before they turn to God. I literally thank God every day that I didn't wait until my life was worse to turn to him.

Thank you for reading my story. There are people who have told me not to put it in my book. *"It will never sell."* Obviously, I didn't listen to their advise. Perhaps, this story is here for you. Maybe, you needed to hear it. Just think about it. Perhaps you are ready to hear what I have said, just like I was ready in that bar after class in December of 1981.

If you are ready, have a talk with God. It doesn't have to be anything special. Just tell him how you feel and that you want this gift that he already wants you to have anyway. Then, tell someone what you have done…someone who may have been talking to you about God for a long time. Believe me there is someone praying for you right now that would be thrilled to hear that you have accepted the gift that God has offered you. If you can't think of anyone to tell, tell me. Send me an e-mail at lagniappe@lindamitchell.net. Or write to me at P.O. Box 987 Union Lake, MI 48387-0987. *I* will be thrilled!

INDEX

REFERENCES

CONTACT INFORMATION FOR COMPANIES AND PEOPLE MENTIONED IN THIS BOOK

1. ABWA—American Business Women's Association
    Visit their website to find an organization near you.
    www.abwa.org

2. John G. Agno—Newsletter Editor & Business Coach
    johnagno@signatureseries.com
    Voice: 734.426.2000
    Fax: 734.426.2109

3. Dr. Tony Alessandra—Personality Profile
    Free on his website
    www.tonyalessandra.com
    Speakers Office, Inc.
    6120 Paseo Del Norte, Ste. B-1
    Carlsbad, CA 92009
    Phone (760) 603-8110
    Fax (760) 603-8010
    Toll Free (800) 222-4383

4. Alpine Industries—
    Ionic Air Purification
    Living Water Filtration System
    www.alpineindustries.com5.

5. Johannes Arnold
    Personal Fitness Coach
    Detroit Metropolitan Area
    248-342-8891

6. Doug Bingham, CFP—
    Certified Financial Planner/Financial Advisor
    Raymond James & Associates, INC
    31550 Northwestern Hwy.
    Farmington Hills, Mi. 48334
    248-932-5450
    dbingham@35n.rjf.com

7. Sadie Bolos
    Keynote Speaker
    Bolos AME, LLC
    586-775-9930

8. Church Study Course
    Various Bible Studies
    127 Ninth Avenue, North
    Nashville, TN 37234

9. Day Runner—www.dayrunner.com

10. Day Timer—www.daytimer.com

11. Barry Demp Coaching, LLC
    200 East Big Beaver
    Suite 136
    Troy, MI 48083
    248-740-3231
    dempcoaching.com

12. Divorce Recovery Information
    Timm Jackson—Pastor

Canyon Creek Community Church
251 N. Roosevelt Avenue
Chandler, AZ 85226
(480) 940-9700
Paul Clough Pastor
Single Pointe Ministries
Ward Presbyterian Church—www.wardepc.org
40000 Six Mile Road
Northville, MI 48167
248-374-7400.

13. Jacque Martin-Downs
    Child Therapist
    Keynote Speaker
    Workshop Leader
    Certified Facilitator for True Colors Personality Styles
    800-940-3808

14. Focus on the Family
    Colorado Springs, CO 80995
    (800) A-Family (232-6459)
    (719) 531-3424 FAX

15. Franklin-Covey Corporate Headquarters
    801-975-1776
    800-827-1776
    www.franklincovey.com
    2200 West Parkway Blvd.
    Salt Lake City, Utah 84119

16. Grace Centers of Hope
    a rehabilitation center for addicted and abused men,
    women and children
    35 E. Huron Street

P.O. Box 420725 Pontiac, MI 48342-0725
www.gracecentersofhope.org

17. Susan Harrow, Media Strategist
Harrow Communications
4200 Park Blvd. 333W
Oakland, CA
510-763-0800
www.prsecrets.com

18. Kari Hunter, LMFT, LCPC
Business & Personal Coaching for Entrepreneurial Couples
(847) 289—1468
Karihunt@aol.com
www.KariHunter.com

19. Ideal Health TM
Fit Test TM (Recommended by Dr. Jack Tips.)
Priva-Test TM (Test for custom supplements)
50 Salem Street
Lynnfield, MA 01940
781-716-2700

20. John Knight
Author of *Change Your Conversation; Change Your Life*
www.JohnKnight.cc

21. Kiwanis Clubs International
Visit their website for a club near you.
www.kiwanis.org

22. Gary Lalonde Corporate Training, Books and Tapes
Premier Performance, Inc.
367 Wales Center Road
Wale, Michigan 48027-3113

Phone: 1-810-325-1182 or 1-800-577-U-CAN
Fax: 1-810-325-1116

23. Vickie Lewis—Author of
Side-by-side:
A Photographic History of American Women in Military Service.
Business Coach
703-379-6270

24. Laurie Lynn Limbers
To obtain the calendar mentioned by Ms. Limbers visit this website www.etrot.org or send a check or money order for $12.00 plus $3.50 shipping and handling to MSBA Calendar, P.O. Box 59, Sand Creek, Michigan 49279.

25. Lifetime Fitness—Family Fitness Centers
Visit their website for a club near you.
www.lifetimefitness.com

26. Mannatech
Metabolic Profile on line at http://www.mannapages.com

27. Dr. Tom McQueen—Author of
Near-Life Experiences:
Discovering New Powers for Personal Growth,
Business Consultant, Keynote Speaker
CorVal, Inc.
5569 Salem Square Drive South
Palm Harbor, FL 34685
800-677-8258

28. Dr. Gail Majcher—Author of *A Worthy Woman*
Call 734-432-3133 to order an autographed copy of the book.

29. Dan Miller—To get a copy of his workbook and tape series ""48 Days to the Work You Love" visit his website at www.48days.com, Toll free 888-373-7771
Dan Miller, P.O.Box 681381, Franklin, TN 37064.

30. Nikken, Inc. Magnetic Therapy and Sleep System
www.nikken.com
949-789-2000
52 Discovery
Irvine, CA

31. Optimist Club International
Visit their website for a club near you.
www.optimist.org

32. Rethinking Marriage While Thinking Remarriage—Information
    ♦ Timm Jackson—Pastor
      Canyon Creek Community Church
      251 N. Roosevelt Avenue
      Chandler, AZ 85226
      (480) 940-9700 www.canyoncreek.org
    ♦ Paul Clough—Pastor Single Pointe Ministries
      Ward Evangelical Presbyterian Church—www.wardepc.org
      40000 Six Mile Road
      Northville, MI 48167
      248-374-7400.

33. Jan Schleicher—Business Coach
Certified Instructor *48 Hours to the Life You Love*
www.tripointperformance.com.

34. Sharper Image—Ionic Air Purification System
www.sharperimage.com

35. Single Pointe Ministries
     Largest Singles Organization in the Country
     Paul Clough
     Ward Presbyterian Church—www.wardepc.org
     40000 Six Mile Road
     Northville, MI 48167
     248-374-7400.

36. SmokEnders—Public and Private Classes, Smoking Cessation
     1 800 828 HELP (4357)
     www.smokenders.com
     901 NW 133rd St. #A
     Vancouver, WA 98685 USA

37. Toastmasters International
     Visit their website for an organization near you.
     www.toastmasters.org

38. 20/20, Barbara Walters and John Stossel
     www.abcnew.go.com/2020

39. Ward Evangelical Presbyterian Church—www.wardepc.org
     40000 Six Mile Road
     Northville, MI 48167
     248-374-7400.

40. Christina Wolf—Freelance Photography
     Capture Your Expressions Photography
     Specializing in on-site photography
     8234 W. Cooley Lake Road.
     Commerce Twp. MI 48382
     248-396-5774
     info@captureyourexpressions.com

BIBLIOGRAPHY

Alter, Judy, *Christopher Reeve: triumph over tragedy*. Danbury, CN: Franklin Watts, c2000.

Bannister, Roger. *The four-minute mile*. New York : Lyons & Burford, 1989.

Beaton, Margaret. *Oprah Winfrey, TV talk show host*. Chicago: Childrens Press, 1990.

Belasco, James A. and Ralph C. Stayer. *Flight of the buffalo: soaring to excellence , learning to let employees lead*. New York: Warner Books, 1994.

Blackaby, Herny T. and King, Claud V. *Experiencing God, a bible study*. Nashville, TN: LifeWay Press, 1990.

Blaiklock, E.M. *Jesus Christ Man or Myth*. Nashville, TN: Thomas Nelson, 1984.

Broome, James with Sandra Aldrich. *The only way back*. Melbourne, FL: Harbor House Publisher, 1990. (Out of print)

Bruner, Kurt D. *Responsible living in an age of excuses*. Chicago: Moody Press, 1992.

165.Canfield, Jack and Mark Victor Hansen. *Chicken soup for the soul*. Deerfield Beach, FL: Health Communications, Inc., 1993.

Canfield, Jack et al. *Chicken soup for the woman's soul,* Deerfield Beach, FL: Health Communications, Inc, 1998.

Carnegie, Dale. *How to win friends and influence people.*New York: Simon and Schuster, 1936.

Covey, Stephen. *Seven habits of highly effective people: powerful lessons in personal change.* New York: Simon and Schuster, 1989.

Gerber, Michael E. *The E-myth revisited: why most small business don't work and what to do about it.* New York: HarperCollins Publishers, Inc. 1995.

Glasser, William. *Reality therapy, a new approach to psychiatry.* With a foreword by O. H. Mowrer. New York: Harper & Row, 1965.

Helmstetter, Shad Ph.D. *What to say when you talk to yourself.*New York: Simon and Schuster, 1982.

Johnson, Spencer. *Who moved my cheese.* New York: G.P. Punam's Sons, 1998.

Jones, Laurie Beth. *The path: creating your mission statement for work and for life.* New York: Hyperion, 1996.

Keirsey, David and Marilyn Bates. *Please understand me, character and temperament types.* DelMar, CA: Gnosology Books Ltd., 1984.

166 Choose Change....167 *Linda Limbers Mitchell* Kriegel, Robert J. and Louis Patler. *If it ain't broke— break it! and other unconventional wisdom for a changing business world.*New York:Warner Books, 1991.

Lewis, Vickie. *Side-by-side: a photographic history of american women in military service.* New York, NY: Stewart, Tabori & Chang, 1999.

Littauer, Florence. *How to get along with difficult people.* Eugene, OR: Harvest House, 1984.

MacDonald, Gordon. *Ordering your private world.* Nashville: T. Nelson Publishers, 1995.

Majcher, Gail. *A worthy woman: my memoirs as a survivor of domestic violence.* Northville, MI: Gail Majcher Publisher, 1998.

McQueen, Tom. *Near life experiences.* Palm Harbor: JEM Publishing, 1997Maxwell, John C. *Developing the leaders around you: how to help others reach their full potential.* Nashville, TN: Thomas Nelson, 1995.

Meyer, Paul. *Don't let jerks get the best of you: advice for dealing with difficult people.* Nashville, TN: Thomas Nelson, Inc. 1993.

McGraw, Phillip C. *Life strategies: doing what works, doing what matters.* New York: Hyperion Books, 1999.

Moore, Beth. *Breaking free.* Nashville, TN: LifeWay Press, 2000.

Murphy, John. *Think change.* Successories Library. (800)535-2773)

Pelzer, Dave. *Help yourself: celebrating the rewards of resilience and gratitude.* New York: Dutton, 2000..Oakley, Ed and Krug, Doug. *Enlightened leadership.* New York: Fireside. 1994.

Reno, Kelly. *The 101 best freelance careers.* New York: The Berkley Publishing Group, 1999.

Richardson, Cheryl. *Take time for your life.* New York: Broadway Books, 1999.

Riley, Pat. *The winner within.* New York: G. P. Putnam's Sons Publishing, 1993.

Schwartz, David J. Ph.D. *The magic of thinking big.* New York: Simon and Schuster, 1987.

Smalley, Gary and John Trent. *love is a decision: ten proven principles to energize your marriage and family.* Dallas : Word Pub., 1989.

Smalley, Gary and John Trent. *The two sides of love: what strengthens affection, closeness, and lasting commitment?* Colorado Springs, CO: Focus on the Family; Dallas: Word Books, 1992.

Smith, Hyrum. *The advanced day planner user guide.* Salt Lake City, UT: Franklin International Institute, Inc. 1987.

Smith, Hyrum. *The 10 natural laws of successful time and life management: proven strategies for increased productivity and inner peace.* New York: Time Warner, 1994.

Swartz, David J. *The magic of thinking big.* New York: Fireside, 1987.

Tips, Jack, CCN. *The weight is over.* Austin, TX: Apple A Day Press, 1999.

Trent, John. *LifeMapping.* Colorado Springs, CO: Focus on the Family Publishing, 1994.

ABOUT THE AUTHOR

Linda Limbers Mitchell has more than twenty years of experience in communication. She is an author, professional trainer, speaker and executive business coach. For the past 12 years Ms. Mitchell has conducted seminars in personal development and change management for clients such as Daimler Chrysler, General Motors and HCR Manor Care. As a highly rated speaker she brings enthusiasm and commitment to her seminars and has the ability to get participants involved. Her warm smile and personal stories put people at ease. Attendees walk away with concrete concepts to improve their lives and the belief that they are capable of making these things happen.

Coaching

Ms. Mitchell has been in private practice as an executive coach for the past eight years. She works with senior level managers and business owners to help clarify their mission/purpose and improve overall performance in the organization. Many clients have found that their ROI for coaching was double their investment and resulted in substantial savings because it took what employees had learned in training programs and insured that it was put into practice.

Presenter/Facilitator

Based on participant feedback, Linda Mitchell has frequently been requested to return as a speaker for professional organizations and corporations around the country. The audiences have ranged from 40 to over 400. In 1979 she became a certified facilitator for Smokenders, the oldest and largest smoking cessation program in the world where she has helped thousands of participants "kick the habit". This is where she discovered an interest in the science of change. From there she has gone on to present and facilitate programs and seminars related to change for organizations such as Daimler Chrysler, General Motors, Professional Development Associates, Fred Pryor Seminars, and Franklin Covey Time Quest (Corporate Program).

Trainer

Ms. Mitchell was one of a select group chosen to be part of one of the largest training initiatives in automotive history. She was a lead trainer and traveled the country delivering this program for three years. She currently delivers training to various groups on communication skills, conflict resolutions and change management.

What coaching clients say about Ms. Mitchell:

♦ "She helped me clarify my objectives and challenged me to excel. I am better at what I do because of the time we spent together." R. Reid, Sales Executive

♦ "Linda is a great sounding board. Her professional and educated approach helped me to focus on what was really important to me. I get more done in less time than I ever have. Hiring her as my coach was one of the best investments I have ever made… and 'investment' is a very important word in my profession!" D. Bingham, Financial Planner

♦ "I appreciate her direct, straight forward style of communicating. It helped me look at things differently. I know I am more focused and have a better idea of what I want to do with the rest of my life." T. McDonald, Health Practitioner

What participants say about Ms. Mitchell:

♦ "Excellent Speaking Skills. Has the ability to get the message across." G. Barlow

- "Terrific. Very positive and upbeat in presentation. Leaves you believing that you can change for the better." L. Wilkins
- "Linda made the seminar exciting. She was informative and well prepared." L. Tanaacea

Please contact Ms. Mitchell for information about coaching and speaking engagements:

Coaches for Life
P. O. Box 987
Union Lake, MI 48387-0987
248-363-6880
info@coachesforlife.com

0-595-20744-8